Table of Contents

ISBN 978-1-60418-255-2

Ready-to-Use Ideas and Activities

This book was developed to help students master the basic skills necessary to become competent readers. The stronger their foundation in reading basics, the faster and easier children will be able to advance to more challenging texts.

Mastering the skills covered within the activity pages of this book is paramount for successful reading comprehension. The activities at the beginning of the book aim to build and reinforce vocabulary, the foundation of reading comprehension. These activities lead to practice with more advanced comprehension skills such as categorizing and using context to understand words. Then, at the end of the book, students begin to practice answering comprehension questions about progressively longer stories.

All children learn at their own rate; therefore, use your judgment to introduce concepts to children when developmentally appropriate.

Hands-On Learning

Hands-on learning reinforces the skills covered within the activity pages and improves students' potential for comprehension. One idea for a hands-on activity is to use the removable flash cards at the back of this book to play a game of bingo. To do this, make a copy of the bingo card on the next page for each student. Write the flash card words on the board and have students choose 24 of the words and write them in the empty spaces of their bingo cards in any order. When students have finished writing on their cards, gather the flash cards into a deck. Call out the words one at a time. Any student who has a word that you call out should make an X through the word on her card to cross it out. The student who crosses out five words in a row first (horizontally, vertically, or diagonally) wins the game by calling out, "Bingo!" To extend the game, you can continue playing until a student crosses out all of the words on his bingo card.

Comprehension Checks and Discussion

In addition to the activities in this book, you can support reading comprehension growth when you read stories in the classroom. After a story—or part of a story—is read, ask your students questions to ensure and enhance reading comprehension. The first type of question you might ask is a factual question. A factual question includes question words such as *who, what, when, where, how,* and *why.* For example, *How old is the character?, Where does the character live?, What time was it when…?,* or any other question that has a clear answer. You might also ask open-ended questions. These types of questions do not have a clear answer. They are based on opinions about the story, not on facts. For example, an open-ended question might be, *Why do you think the character acted as he did?, How do you think the character felt about her actions or the actions of others?, What do you think the character will do next?,* or *What other ways could this story have ended?*

Vocabulary Bingo

		FREE		

et and *est*

Fill in the blank with the word that makes the most sense in the sentence.

bet	net	pet	set	vet	wet

1. Lucas has a _____ rabbit.

2. We had to take our sick dog to the _____.

3. My stepdad hit a tennis ball over the _____.

4. Please _____ the dishes on the table.

5. I _____ my brother will sleep late tomorrow.

6. Hope's hair was _____ after she washed it.

best	nest	pest	quest	vest	west

1. The birds made a _____ in the tree.

2. I wore my favorite _____ to school.

3. Sam is on a _____ to find his book.

4. My family drove from east to _____ last summer.

5. The bee was a _____ buzzing around Shara's head.

6. I got the _____ math grade in the class.

ight and *ive*

Fill in the blank with the word that makes the most sense in the sentence.

bright	flight	light	night	sight	tight

1. We took a _____ on an airplane to see Grandma.

2. Casey's old shoes are too _____ to wear.

3. Our eyes give us the sense of _____.

4. Hilda shined the _____ flashlight on the ground.

5. At bedtime, Mom tells us "Good _____."

6. The empty box was very _____ to carry.

arrive	dive	drive	five	hive	live

1. What time should we _____ for the party?

2. Zach and Katie saw their favorite singer _____ in concert.

3. I like to _____ into the deep pool.

4. The human body has _____ senses.

5. The bees buzzed around their _____.

6. Aunt Sharon will _____ us to the game.

ay and *ash*

Fill in the blank with the word that makes the most sense in the sentence.

| stay | day | hay | may | ray | tray |

1. Mom, _____ I have some more grapes, please?

2. Horses like to eat _____.

3. Please take the _____ of food to your table.

4. A _____ of light shined on my pillow.

5. Rita wants to _____ at the park and play.

6. Friday is Anne's favorite _____ of the week.

| splash | dash | flash | mash | cash | trash |

1. Bill likes to _____ in the water.

2. Please take out the _____.

3. A _____ of lightning lit the sky.

4. Carlos paid _____ for his lunch.

5. Jill won the 50-yard _____.

6. Dad will _____ potatoes for dinner.

Name _____

ain and *age*

Fill in the blank with the word that makes the most sense in the sentence.

brain	gain	grain	main	pain	train

1. When my arm broke, I was in _____.

2. Bread is made from _____.

3. I use my _____ to spell words.

4. The _____ was late to the station.

5. As the puppy eats more, he will _____ weight.

6. Shawna lives on the _____ road into town.

cage	page	sage	age	stage	wage

1. My mother likes to cook with _____.

2. The actors stood on the _____.

3. Your _____ tells how old you are.

4. Anna's job pays a good _____.

5. Turn the _____ and begin reading the next chapter.

6. The bird was in a _____.

amp and *ump*

Fill in the blank with the word that makes the most sense in the sentence.

camp	damp	lamp	ramp	stamp	champ

1. I put a _____ on my letter.

2. Susan wheeled herself up the _____.

3. The rain made the grass _____.

4. We love to _____ by the river.

5. Uncle Marvin turned on the _____ for more light.

6. The fastest runner became the _____.

bump	dump	jump	clump	pump	stump

1. My friend can _____ high.

2. Julie put a _____ of grapes on her dinner plate.

3. We took the trash to the city _____.

4. Cecilia used a _____ to put air in her bike tires.

5. Watch out for the _____ in the road.

6. The woodsman cut down the tree and left a _____.

eam and ow

Fill in the blank with the word that makes the most sense in the sentence.

| beam | cream | dream | gleam | steam | team |

1. The boiling water turned into _____.

2. My teeth always _____ after I visit the dentist.

3. Our _____ won the third race.

4. The flashlight _____ was very bright.

5. Juan's _____ is to become a teacher.

6. We had ice _____ with our cake.

| bow | cow | plow | how | now | wow |

1. The farmer had to _____ the field.

2. This milk comes from a _____.

3. Yesterday, Erin was tired, but _____, she is rested.

4. The actors took a _____.

5. George showed me _____ to boil eggs.

6. _____! What a great job you did.

ake and *ack*

Fill in the blank with the word that makes the most sense in the sentence.

brake	flake	lake	make	rake	wake

1. I caught a _____ of snow in my hand.

2. Joseph showed me how to use the _____ on my bike.

3. June and Jude went fishing at the _____.

4. Sometimes, it is hard to _____ up in the morning.

5. Mom wants to _____ pizza after school.

6. Maria likes to _____ the yard.

back	black	snack	pack	rack	sack

1. We have a _____ cat.

2. Ben helped put the food in a _____ at the store.

3. The three boys sit at the _____ of the bus.

4. I am hungry for a _____.

5. My stepmom will _____ our car for the trip.

6. Please put the dishes on the _____ to dry.

CD-104305 • © Carson-Dellosa

Name _____

ip and op

Fill in the blank with the word that makes the most sense in the sentence.

clip	drip	flip	sip	snip	trip

1. My dad can _____ the pancakes in the pan.

2. Melting ice will _____ in your hand.

3. Julio will _____ the papers together.

4. The kitten likes to _____ milk.

5. Jessica used scissors to _____ the thread.

6. I am going on a _____ to see Grandpa.

crop	drop	flop	mop	pop	stop

1. When I am tired, I _____ onto my bed and rest.

2. I _____ at the crosswalk and look both ways.

3. A _____ of water fell into the sink.

4. The farmer planted his _____ of wheat.

5. Charlotte needed to _____ up the spill.

6. Please do not _____ my balloon.

Name _____

ace and *are*

Fill in the blank with the word that makes the most sense in the sentence.

face	pace	place	race	space	trace

1. Mei walked away at a quick _____.

2. Someday, I want to go to outer _____.

3. At bedtime, you should wash your _____.

4. My uncle won his first _____.

5. Go back to the _____ you started.

6. Angelo did not leave a _____ of food on his plate.

bare	care	fare	hare	dare	mare

1. We paid our _____ on the train.

2. A _____ is like a rabbit.

3. Don't you _____ touch that stove!

4. My brother likes to take _____ of things.

5. Please keep your _____ feet off the furniture.

6. A female horse is called a _____.

Name _____

eck and ind

Fill in the blank with the word that makes the most sense in the sentence.

check	deck	neck	peck	speck	fleck

1. My cat has a white _____ on her left paw.

2. Put a _____ next to the correct answer.

3. There is a _____ of dirt on my shirt.

4. The bird likes to _____ at its food.

5. Your _____ is between your head and shoulders.

6. Captain Smith stood on the _____ of the ship.

behind	blind	find	kind	rind	wind

1. Sasha is _____, yet she is an amazing piano player.

2. Always be _____ to your neighbors.

3. Let me help you _____ your keys.

4. The teacher stood _____ the class for the photograph.

5. Liam peeled the _____ off of his orange.

6. Grandpa has to _____ his watch.

Compound words are two words that have been put together to make a new word. For example, *flash* and *light* can be put together to make the new word *flashlight*. Look at the list of compound words. Fill in each blank in the stories below with the best compound word. Use each word once.

classroom	lunchtime	backpack	seesaw
breakfast	playground	popcorn	homework

My School Day

Mom wakes me up to get dressed and eat _____. I pack my

_____ and go to school. I work at my desk in the _____. When

it is _____, I sit with my friends. At recess, we go to the _____.

We like to play on the _____. At the end of the day, our teacher writes our

_____ on the board. After school, I like to eat _____ for a snack.

· ·

nighttime	outside	lunchtime	backyard
doghouse	nutshells	butterfly	weekend

Weekend Fun

I like the _____ because I get to spend time _____ with my

dog Rusty. In the morning, Rusty comes out of his _____ to play. We play in the

_____ until _____. Rusty likes to bark at the

_____ that lives in the garden. He also likes to chew on the _____

that squirrels have dropped from the trees. When _____ comes, Rusty and I are

ready to sleep!

Name _____

Compound words are two words that have been put together to make a new word. For example, *in* and *side* can be put together to make the new word *inside*. Look at the list of compound words. Fill in each blank in the stories below with the best compound word. Use each word once.

washtub	pancakes	upbeat	goldfish
everything	grandmother	summertime	bedtime

My Grandmother

I like it when my _____ comes to stay with me in the _____.

She is an _____ person. She knows how to make _____ fun. She

tells me stories while we make _____ in the morning. We splash each other when

she shows me how to wash clothes in a _____. She sings funny songs while we feed

my _____. Grandmother even knows games that make _____ fun!

. . . .

touchdown	football	kneepads	overtime
newspaper	sometimes	headgear	kickoff

Football

My brother is on the _____ team. He wears special _____ and

_____ to keep his body safe. I go to watch his games _____. It is

fun to watch the _____ at the beginning of the game. One day, the game went into

_____ and they had to play longer. My brother scored the winning

_____! The next day, his picture was in the _____!

Compound words are two words that have been put together to make a new word. For example, *when* and *ever* can be put together to make the new word *whenever*. Look at the list of compound words. Fill in each blank in the stories below with the best compound word. Use each word once.

grasshoppers	ladybugs	lunchtime	tablecloth
watermelon	hamburgers	outside	sunglasses

Picnic

My family loves to go _____ and have a picnic. Mom spreads out the

_____ on the ground. At _____, Dad serves us

_____. We eat _____ for dessert. We watch

_____ and _____ move through the grass. I put on my

_____ and play with my sister.

sandbox	storybook	bookshelf	afternoon
oatmeal	bumblebee	bedroom	naptime

Little Sister

My little sister is fun to take care of. She likes to eat _____ for breakfast. In the

_____, she likes to play in her _____. She gets tired and comes in

for _____. I take a _____ off the _____ and read

to her. Her favorite story is about a _____. After the story, she goes to sleep in her

_____.

CD-104305 • © Carson-Dellosa

Name _____

Compound words are two words that have been put together to make a new word. For example, *thumb* and *print* can be put together to make the new word *thumbprint*. Look at the list of compound words. Fill in each blank in the stories below with the best compound word. Use each word once.

necktie	raincoats	earrings	necklace
briefcase	stepmom	everyone	shoelaces

Getting Ready for the Day

_____ in my family gets ready for the day in a different way. My

_____ puts on her jewelry, like her _____ and a

_____. Dad puts on a _____ and picks up his

_____ to take to work. I just tie my _____, and I am ready to go!

When the weather is bad, we all do one thing the same. We all put on our _____!

. . . .

suitcases	airport	takeoff	gumball
doorway	seatbelt	headphones	airplane

Flying

Last year, Mom and I flew to visit Grandpa. We got to the _____ early and put

tags on our _____. When the _____ arrived, we got in line to

board. We walked through the _____ of the plane and found our seats. I put on my

_____, and Mom gave me some _____ so I could listen to music.

After _____, my ears hurt a little, so Mom gave me a _____

to chew.

Name _____

Compound words are two words that have been put together to make a new word. For example, *over* and *coat* can be put together to make the new word *overcoat*. Look at the list of compound words. Fill in each blank in the stories below with the best compound word. Use each word once.

| butterflies | earthworms | backyard | ladybugs |
| fireflies | honeybees | everywhere | rainstorm |

Insects

Bugs are _____ you look. _____ like to get pollen from flowers. _____ have colorful wings. _____ are red with black spots. _____ live in the ground and come out after a _____. When it is dark, _____ come out and fly around. It is fun to see them light up in the _____.

| underwater | fishhook | catfish | campfire |
| rowboat | sunshine | something | waterproof |

Fishing

My uncle likes to go fishing. He puts on old clothes and _____ boots and stands by the water. Sometimes, he goes out in a _____. He puts bait on the _____ and throws out the line. The hook sinks _____. He waits for the _____ swimming to take the bait. He stands in the _____ and fishes until he catches _____. Then, he cooks the fish over a _____.

CD-104305 • © Carson-Dellosa

Name _____

Compound words are two words that have been put together to make a new word. For example, *eye* and *lid* can be put together to make the new word *eyelid*. Look at the list of compound words. Fill in each blank in the stories below with the best compound word. Use each word once.

rainstorms	rainwater	weatherman	snowflakes
snowstorms	rainfall	snowmen	thunderclouds

Rain and Snow

The _____ tells us what weather we can expect. In the spring, we usually

have _____ with lots of dark _____. Our garden needs the

_____, and we like to collect _____ to water our plants with

later. During winter, we usually get _____! We watch the white

_____ fall. Later, we go outside and play in the snow. We even make

_____!

. . . .

someday	shoemaker	schoolteacher	firefighter
anything	hairdresser	lawmaker	salesperson

Jobs

What job would you like to have _____ when you are an adult? A

_____ makes and fixes shoes. A _____ works with children.

A _____ cuts people's hair. Both a police officer and a _____

help people. A _____ sells things. A _____ works in an office.

Girls and boys can be _____ they choose!

Rooms

Look at the list of words below. Write each word where it is most commonly found.

apron	nightstand	stove	sink
flour	toys	dresser	blanket
sheet	grill	clothes	cup
slippers	fork	dishwasher	bookcase
mixer	bathrobe	glass	spoon
pajamas	teapot	clock	hangers

Bedroom   **Kitchen**

_____   _____

_____   _____

_____   _____

_____   _____

_____   _____

_____   _____

_____   _____

_____   _____

_____   _____

_____   _____

Name _____

Animals

Look at the list of words below. Write each word where it is most commonly found.

kitten	zebra	lion	tiger
goldfish	gerbil	hamster	monkey
alligator	ferret	puppy	mouse
gorilla	kangaroo	bird	elephant
penguin	rabbit	shark	turtle
cat	bear	dog	giraffe

Pets

Zoo Animals

_____ _____

_____ _____

_____ _____

_____ _____

_____ _____

_____ _____

_____ _____

_____ _____

_____ _____

Food

Look at the list of words below. Write each word where it is most commonly found.

eggs	soup	pizza	jelly
fish	rice	waffle	juice
toast	roll	oatmeal	fruit
sausage	bagel	carrots	salad
pancakes	peas	pickles	dumplings
milk	corn	cereal	beans

Breakfast   **Dinner**

_____   _____

_____   _____

_____   _____

_____   _____

_____   _____

_____   _____

_____   _____

_____   _____

_____   _____

_____   _____

Name _____

Time

Look at the list of words below. Write each word in the correct list.

sunlight	moonlight	stars	noon
midnight	bedtime	sleep	awake
school	night-light	breakfast	dinner
sunrise	sunset	lunch	sunny
dark	picnic	dusk	dawn
sundown	dream	daylight	work

Day   **Night**

_____   _____

_____   _____

_____   _____

_____   _____

_____   _____

_____   _____

_____   _____

_____   _____

_____   _____

_____   _____

Name _____

Weather

Look at the list of words below. Write each word in the correct list.

umbrella	snowman	skiing	thunder	lightning
bright	hot	cold	wet	snowball
dry	sprinkle	drops	flakes	icy
puddle	clouds	sun	sunglasses	winter
summer	splash	mittens	swimming	raincoat
clear	shining	blazing	arctic	shovel

Sunny

Snowy

Rainy

_____

_____

_____

_____

_____

_____

_____

_____

_____

_____

_____

_____

_____

_____

_____

_____

_____

_____

_____

_____

_____

_____

_____

_____

Name _____

Senses

Look at the list of words below. Write each word in the correct list.

eyes	nose	ears	scent	hear
see	perfume	flower	cookies	picture
radio	television	movie	concert	barking
crying	odor	song	voice	glasses
skunk	loud	yellow	noise	eyelid
watch	lemon	view	trash	soap

Sight	**Sound**	**Smell**
_____	_____	_____
_____	_____	_____
_____	_____	_____
_____	_____	_____
_____	_____	_____
_____	_____	_____
_____	_____	_____
_____	_____	_____
_____	_____	_____

Sports

Look at the list of words below. Write each word in the correct list.

pool	glove	bases	kick	field
mound	bat	swimsuit	goggles	team
water	ball	pitcher	score	dive
throw	underwater	slide	goal	float
coach	pass	goalie	dugout	

Swimming	Soccer	Baseball
_____	_____	_____
_____	_____	_____
_____	_____	_____
_____	_____	_____
_____	_____	_____
_____	_____	_____
_____	_____	_____

CD-104305 • © Carson-Dellosa

Name _____

Homophones

Homophones are words that sound alike but are spelled differently. The words also mean different things. Choose the correct homophone for each sentence.

bare	bear	heel	heal	tale	tail

1. Joey hurt the _____ of his foot when he stepped on a stone.

2. My favorite _____ is the story about Jack and the giant.

3. A _____ lives in the woods and likes to eat honey.

4. Doctors try to _____ people.

5. Kurt stuck his _____ feet in the swimming pool.

6. Her dog wags its _____ when it is happy.

fair	fare	maid	made	weak	week

1. My family went to the state _____.

2. What is your favorite day of the _____?

3. A _____ is someone who helps with cleaning and serving.

4. After Uma won the race, her legs felt _____.

5. The bus _____ is one dollar.

6. Julia _____ a picture frame for her stepdad.

Name _____

Homophones

Homophones are words that sound alike but are spelled differently. The words also mean different things. Choose the correct homophone for each sentence.

too	two	to	cent	scent	sent

1. The _____ kittens played with the ball of yarn.

2. A penny equals one _____.

3. My aunt asked me to go _____ the store.

4. Malcolm _____ a letter to his friend.

5. I will clean my desk and the table _____.

6. The flower has a sweet _____.

I	eye	you	ewe	wear	where

1. My friend and _____ ate lunch together.

2. The _____ took care of her lamb.

3. You can see many things with your _____.

4. Do you know _____ to put the books away?

5. Would _____ please hand me that pencil?

6. Hillary will _____ her blue shoes today.

 CD-104305 • © Carson-Dellosa

Homophones

Homophones are words that sound alike but are spelled differently. The words also mean different things. Choose the correct homophone for each sentence.

bury	berry	hare	hair	ate	eight

1. Jen will be _____ years old tomorrow.

2. Mom put a fresh _____ in each glass of lemonade.

3. Some people _____ dinner before they went to the game.

4. In the story, the fox and the _____ had a race.

5. Our dog likes to _____ the bones we give him.

6. Mark's sister has long brown _____.

main	mane	wrap	rap	four	for

1. The horse's _____ was hard to brush.

2. Please _____ the gift in pretty paper.

3. I have _____ people in my family.

4. Dad went _____ a walk in the park.

5. We heard a _____ at the door.

6. Dave lives on the _____ road in his town.

Homophones

Homophones are words that sound alike but are spelled differently. The words also mean different things. Choose the correct homophone for each sentence.

one	won	here	hear	hire	higher

1. We are _____ to learn.

2. My brother hopes they _____ him for the job.

3. David had _____ sticker left, and he gave it to his friend.

4. The plane flew _____ than the kite.

5. Do you _____ a band playing music?

6. Chan ran fast and _____ the race.

know	no	meet	meat	pause	paws

1. My cat washes her face using her _____.

2. Maria added _____ to the taco.

3. Did you _____ that ice is frozen water?

4. The students will _____ after school to play games.

5. Please _____ so I do not miss anything.

6. There are _____ apples left on the tree.

Name _____

Homophones

Homophones are words that sound alike but are spelled differently. The words also mean different things. Choose the correct homophone for each sentence.

course	coarse	groan	grown	rose	rows

1. My uncle's beard is very _____.

2. When I am fully _____, I want to be a nurse.

3. Larry gave his stepmom a _____ for her birthday.

4. The pain in my leg made me _____.

5. The farmer planted 10 new _____ of corn.

6. Of _____ you may have more soup!

stare	stair	read	red	pail	pale

1. I sat on the bottom _____ in front of the building.

2. I used a _____ and sand to make a sand castle.

3. Our teacher _____ a story to us after lunch.

4. The light brown chair looked _____ next to the dark brown chair.

5. My cat likes to _____ out the window.

6. Ling wore a bright _____ dress in the play.

Name _____

Homophones

Homophones are words that sound alike but are spelled differently. The words also mean different things. Choose the correct homophone for each sentence.

right	write	sail	sale	root	route

1. The _____ of a tooth is below the gum.

2. Mark the _____ answer on your paper.

3. Captain Juan will _____ the boat to shore.

4. The sign says that the car is for _____.

5. Lilly liked taking the faster _____ to school.

6. I will _____ a story about my town.

our	hour	side	sighed	weather	whether

1. We will be home in an _____.

2. The _____ is beautiful today!

3. Taylor _____ when she sat in her chair.

4. My family loves _____ house.

5. Sheila painted one _____ of the fence purple.

6. Harry wondered _____ or not he should take an umbrella.

Name _____

Homophones

Homophones are words that sound alike but are spelled differently. The words also mean different things. Choose the correct homophone for each sentence.

due	do	dew	seize	seas	sees

1. The fisherman sailed the seven _____.

2. A fun thing to _____ is to visit the creek.

3. Sherry's library book is _____ on Monday.

4. Josh _____ his grandparents every weekend.

5. When you _____ something, you grab it.

6. We smelled the morning _____ in the air.

pair	pare	pear	rain	reign	rein

1. The king will _____ for his whole life.

2. When you have a _____ of something, you have two of them.

3. The cool _____ felt good on our hot faces.

4. To make the horse slow down, pull on the _____.

5. Would you like an apple or a _____?

6. Mom will _____ the potatoes before cooking them.

Using Context Clues

When you come to a word and you do not know the meaning, use context clues to help you figure it out. Context clues are the other words around the word you do not know.

Use context clues to figure out the meaning of each underlined word below. Circle the correct meaning.

1. My brother and I often argue about who gets to use the computer.

    a. work   b. disagree   c. study

2. The official told us not to enter the building until 8 o'clock.

    a. person in charge   b. nurse   c. child

3. Josie saw an unusual light in the sky and asked her teacher what it was.

    a. dark   b. star   c. different

4. The cardinal in my backyard is a beautiful sight. I love its bright color and sweet song.

    a. singer   b. branch   c. bird with red feathers

5. Mom asked me to turn down the volume on the radio because it was too loud.

    a. noise level   b. book   c. color

6. You will need to separate the reading papers from the math papers.

    a. put together   b. set apart   c. teach

7. It is hard to balance in the middle of a seesaw without falling off.

    a. ride   b. stay steady   c. walk

8. If you soak a raisin in water overnight, it will swell to the size of a grape.

    a. grow   b. drown   c. wonderful

 CD-104305 • © Carson-Dellosa

Using Context Clues

When you come to a word and you do not know the meaning, use context clues to help you figure it out. Context clues are the other words around the word you do not know.

Use context clues to figure out the meaning of each underlined word below. Circle the correct meaning.

1. My style is to wear T-shirts and jeans, but my sister wears fancy dresses.

   a. clothes   b. fashion   c. boots

2. I avoid eating snacks before dinnertime.

   a. stay away from   b. love   c. try to have

3. Lucy's family permits her to walk home with a friend.

   a. bans   b. drives   c. allows

4. The journey from my house to Grandma's takes five hours.

   a. trip   b. airplane   c. car

5. My brother built a model airplane. Then, he painted it red and blue.

   a. real   b. person who shows off clothes   c. toy

6. Everyone loves her friendliness and charm.

   a. voice   b. nice manner   c. necklace

7. Please notify the coach today if you would like to try out for the team.

   a. tell   b. obey   c. play for

8. One element of a successful day is getting enough sleep.

   a. start   b. chemical   c. part

Using Context Clues

When you come to a word and you do not know the meaning, use context clues to help you figure it out. Context clues are the other words around the word you do not know.

Use context clues to figure out the meaning of each underlined word below. Circle the correct meaning.

1. The car tire scraped the <u>curb</u> as it went around the corner.

    a. edge of a road   b. sidewalk   c. boots

2. We went on a <u>march</u> through the neighborhood.

    a. month   b. band   c. walk

3. After Jerry ate the <u>entire</u> pizza, his stomach hurt.

    a. whole   b. wheel   c. small

4. Polar bears live in <u>arctic</u> weather.

    a. very hot   b. rainy   c. very cold

5. My stepmom is helping me study so I can <u>improve</u> my grades.

    a. study   b. raise   c. read

6. My teacher invites families to <u>observe</u> her class so that they know how she teaches.

    a. watch   b. leave   c. teach

7. The <u>motion</u> of the rocking boat made me feel ill.

    a. ocean   b. captain   c. movement

8. The motor is at the <u>rear</u> of the boat, just behind the seats.

    a. side   b. back   c. middle

Using Context Clues

When you come to a word and you do not know the meaning, use context clues to help you figure it out. Context clues are the other words around the word you do not know.

Use context clues to figure out the meaning of each underlined word below. Circle the correct meaning.

1. The principal reason for studying is to learn new things.

   a. main   b. school   c. last

2. The teacher will accept our homework until tomorrow morning.

   a. stay away from   b. give away   c. take

3. We tried all morning, but it was impossible to get tickets to the game.

   a. certain   b. easy   c. not possible

4. Mr. Loy told us the good news with a grin on his face.

   a. cheerful   b. smile   c. sad

5. Joey put the photograph in a silver frame.

   a. picture holder   b. question   c. snapshot

6. What is your individual opinion about the food?

   a. class   b. own   c. thought

7. My uncle is a soldier in the military.

   a. armed forces   b. officer   c. government

8. Corrie chose the ordinary name Spot for her Dalmatian puppy.

   a. unusual   b. normal   c. correct

Using Context Clues

When you come to a word and you do not know the meaning, use context clues to help you figure it out. Context clues are the other words around the word you do not know.

Use context clues to figure out the meaning of each underlined word below. Circle the correct meaning.

1. Marcy wanted to <u>magnify</u> the words on the bottle so that she could see them better.

   a. make bigger   b. copy   c. read

2. Each person is wearing a <u>label</u> with his or her name on it.

   a. jacket   b. shirt   c. tag

3. It is not nice to <u>tease</u> people or animals.

   a. obey   b. talk to   c. bother

4. When water is heated, <u>steam</u> rises into the air.

   a. droplets   b. ice   c. lakes

5. Mr. Jones <u>conducts</u> the choir when they give a concert.

   a. behavior   b. leads   c. does experiments

6. It is always nice to see a <u>familiar</u> face.

   a. unknown   b. belonging to parents   c. something that is known

7. Our school's teachers want to <u>educate</u> all of their students.

   a. teach   b. study   c. watch

8. It is always best to be <u>honest</u> in what you do and say.

   a. be funny   b. tell the truth   c. lie about

Name _____

Using Context Clues

When you come to a word and you do not know the meaning, use context clues to help you figure it out. Context clues are the other words around the word you do not know.

Use context clues to figure out the meaning of each underlined word below. Circle the correct meaning.

1. In North America, people vote to elect their leaders of government.
    a. object to   b. choose   c. win

2. The majority of the class voted to have pizza instead of sandwiches for lunch.
    a. most people   b. few people   c. teachers

3. My mom's greatest concern is that we get home safely.
    a. rule   b. problem   c. worry

4. A bride often wears a veil on her head during a wedding.
    a. net that goes over the face   b. long gown   c. flowers

5. You should always be civil to other students and teachers.
    a. quiet   b. rude   c. polite

6. The new pool is private. Only people who live in that neighborhood can use it.
    a. open   b. not public   c. fun

7. The scent of some flowers makes my nose itch.
    a. sound   b. sight   c. smell

8. I will wrap a gift for Mario to open at his party.
    a. buy   b. speak about   c. put paper around

Name _____

Using Context Clues

When you come to a word and you do not know the meaning, use context clues to help you figure it out. Context clues are the other words around the word you do not know.

Use context clues to figure out the meaning of each underlined word below. Circle the correct meaning.

1. The underwater current can be very strong in the ocean.
    a. breeze   b. beach   c. flow

2. We thought long and hard before making a decision.
    a. argument   b. choice   c. lesson

3. Everyone at the party was very merry.
    a. happy   b. upset   c. small

4. Our teacher will display the class poster for the rest of the school to see.
    a. tear up   b. throw away   c. show

5. After a brief speech from one of the actors, the play began.
    a. quiet   b. short   c. noisy

6. The baby seized the rattle his mom was holding and waved it around.
    a. hit   b. stared at   c. grabbed

7. My cat likes to stare out the window.
    a. watch   b. step   c. bother

8. Mike's dog likes to bury everything in a pile of dirt in the backyard.
    a. eat   b. cover   c. play with

Using Context Clues

When you come to a word and you do not know the meaning, use context clues to help you figure it out. Context clues are the other words around the word you do not know.

Use context clues to figure out the meaning of each underlined word below. Circle the correct meaning.

1. Before it rains, I can feel the moisture in the air.
   a. thunder   b. sunshine   c. wetness

2. The bark on a tree is very rough.
   a. outer covering   b. leaves   c. sand

3. I groaned when I realized that I had forgotten my book.
   a. shouted   b. whispered   c. sighed loudly

4. My sister beamed when our mother said, "Good job!"
   a. shined a ray of light   b. smiled broadly   c. frowned

5. The fare for riding the train was a dollar for adults.
   a. ticket price   b. store   c. railroad

6. The crowd rumbled like thunder as the news spread.
   a. jumped   b. screamed   c. roared

7. My hand felt weak after I finished writing the report.
   a. strong   b. tired   c. loose

8. The effect of staying up all night was that I fell asleep at breakfast.
   a. result   b. cause   c. change

Using Context Clues

When you come to a word and you do not know the meaning, use context clues to help you figure it out. Context clues are the other words around the word you do not know.

Use context clues to figure out the meaning of each underlined word below. Circle the correct meaning.

1. Dad likes to make a special tomato sauce to put on our pizza.

    a. bowl   b. dinner   c. topping

2. Drop the noodles into the pan when the water starts to boil.

    a. stir   b. heat   c. freeze

3. My mom and stepdad had to sign a special form to buy our house.

    a. paper   b. book   c. name

4. After I finished eating, my plate was bare.

    a. large animal   b. empty   c. plenty

5. I like wearing skirts because they are pretty when I twirl.

    a. spin   b. don't like   c. enjoy

6. The surface of the water was calm until it began to rain.

    a. stormy   b. still   c. wavy

7. Jimmy liked the glory of winning the city's big race.

    a. honor   b. flag   c. medal

8. My friend and I are opposites, but we still have fun together.

    a. happy   b. exactly alike   c. not alike

Using Context Clues

When you come to a word and you do not know the meaning, use context clues to help you figure it out. Context clues are the other words around the word you do not know.

Use context clues to figure out the meaning of each underlined word below. Circle the correct meaning.

1. Shelby is on a quest to find her watch.

   a. wheel   b. race   c. search

2. Two world wars were fought during the 20th century.

   a. season   b. period of 100 years   c. month

3. The first 13 U.S. states formed a union so that they could be stronger.

   a. separation   b. president   c. single governing body

4. In the story, the fox chased the hare across the field.

   a. rabbit   b. frog   c. something on your head

5. In our society, everyone must follow certain laws.

   a. house   b. community   c. rules

6. Todd ate lunch in the pause between speakers.

   a. break   b. animals' feet   c. nap

7. Anna exclaimed in a loud voice, "I got an A on the test!"

   a. sang   b. read   c. shouted

8. James glanced at my friend across the classroom.

   a. words   b. looked   c. spoke

Name _____

Read the story. Then, answer the questions.

Amelia Earhart

Amelia Earhart is famous for being the first woman to fly an airplane across the Atlantic Ocean. She was born in 1897 and saw her first airplane at the Iowa state fair at age 10. Although she studied to be a nurse and then a social worker, she was always interested in flight. She started taking flying lessons in 1921 and then bought her first plane. Since the aircraft was bright yellow, she called it Canary. In 1928, Earhart flew from Canada to Wales, crossing the Atlantic Ocean in only 21 hours. When she returned to the United States, a parade was held in her honor. She crossed the Atlantic again in 1932, this time by herself. After this accomplishment, the U.S. Congress gave her a special medal called the Distinguished Flying Cross. Earhart continued to set new records, and in 1937 she decided to fly around the world. Her plane was lost over the Pacific Ocean, and Earhart was never heard from again.

1. What is the main idea of this story?
   a. Amelia Earhart flew around the world.
   b. Amelia Earhart was a brave woman who flew airplanes.
   c. Amelia Earhart had a yellow plane called Canary.

2. When was Earhart born?

   _____

3. Where did Earhart see her first airplane?

   _____

4. Why did Earhart call her first plane Canary?

   _____

5. Why did Earhart receive a medal?

   _____

   _____

6. What happened to Earhart in 1937?

   _____

   _____

Name _____

Read the story. Then, answer the questions.

Thomas Jefferson

Thomas Jefferson was an important figure in early U.S. history. He was born in 1743 in the colony of Virginia. He became a lawyer and then grew active in the government of the new country that would become the United States. In 1776, he helped write the U.S. Declaration of Independence, which said that the American colonies were no longer tied to Great Britain. He served as governor of Virginia and then went to France to help strengthen ties between the two countries. Jefferson became the third president of the United States and served two terms from 1801 to 1809. During his presidency, Jefferson authorized the Louisiana Purchase, which expanded U.S. territory to include over 800,000 square miles from Canada to the Gulf Coast. Jefferson died in 1826, but people in the United States are reminded of him every time they spend a nickel. Jefferson's face is on one side, and his home, Monticello, is on the other.

1. What is the main idea of this story?
    a. Thomas Jefferson was an important person in U.S. history.
    b. Thomas Jefferson's face is on the nickel.
    c. Thomas Jefferson was a lawyer.

2. Where was Jefferson born?

   _____

3. What did Jefferson do in 1776?

   _____

4. Why did Jefferson go to France?

   _____

5. When did Jefferson serve as president of the United States?

   _____

6. How did the Louisiana Purchase change the United States?

   _____

   _____

Name _____

Read the story. Then, answer the questions.

Sandford Fleming

What time is it? Before the work of Sandford Fleming, it could be hard to tell. Fleming was born in Scotland in 1827. He moved to Canada, where he drew up plans for a railroad from the east coast to the west coast. He worked to promote the use of iron bridges rather than wood because he thought iron bridges were safer. In 1851, he designed the first Canadian postage stamp, which was worth three cents and had a picture of a beaver on it. In 1876, Fleming was traveling in Ireland when he missed his train. The schedule said that the train would leave at 11 o'clock in the evening, but it left at 11 o'clock in the morning instead. To avoid this kind of problem, Fleming suggested that countries around the world use a single 24-hour clock. By 1929, most of the world's countries had adopted time zones that fit into this measurement of time.

1. What is the main idea of this story?
   a. Sandford Fleming was Scottish but lived in Canada.
   b. Sandford Fleming came up with the idea for standardized time.
   c. Sandford Fleming missed a train in Ireland.

2. What did Fleming draw up plans for in Canada?

   _____

3. Why did Fleming prefer iron bridges to wooden ones?

   _____

4. What did the first Canadian stamp look like?

   _____

5. Why did Fleming miss his train?

   _____

   _____

6. How did Fleming's ideas change the way people tell time today?

   _____

   _____

Name _____

Read the story. Then, answer the questions.

Alexander Graham Bell

Alexander Graham Bell is known as the inventor of the telephone. He was born in 1847 in Edinburgh, Scotland. At the age of 12, after his mother lost her hearing, Bell became interested in studying sound. Bell learned to use sign language so that he could talk to her. He traveled to the United States as an adult and worked as a teacher for people who could not hear. He conducted experiments on how sound travels, which led to his invention of the telephone. In 1876, he was able to speak into one end of his machine. His assistant, Thomas Watson, heard him at the other end, even though he was in another room. The first sentence spoken over the telephone was, "Mr. Watson, come here, I want to see you." The Bell Telephone Company was created shortly afterward, and by 1886 there were over 150,000 phones in use in the United States. Bell died in 1922, but his invention lives on today.

1. What is the main idea of this story?
   a. Thomas Watson was Bell's assistant.
   b. The first telephone call was made in 1876.
   c. Alexander Graham Bell invented the telephone.

2. When was Bell born?

   _____

3. Why was Bell interested in studying sound?

   _____

4. What led to Bell's invention of the telephone?

   _____

5. What was the first sentence said on a telephone?

   _____

6. What can you conclude about how Bell's invention helped people talk to each other?

   _____

   _____

Name _____

Read the story. Then, answer the questions.

Martin Luther King, Jr.

Martin Luther King, Jr., was an important leader in the U.S. civil rights movement. The civil rights movement forced leaders to change laws so that all people would be treated fairly, regardless of their skin color. King was born in 1929 in Atlanta, Georgia. In 1954, King became the leader of a church in Montgomery, Alabama. During this time, African Americans were told that they had to give up their bus seats if a white person wanted to sit down. King and others refused to ride the buses at all until they were given equal treatment. In 1963, he led a march in Washington, D.C., to ask the government to change the laws so that everyone was treated fairly. King received the Nobel Peace Prize in 1964 for his work. He traveled to Memphis, Tennessee, in 1968 to give a speech in support of equal wages. He was shot on April 4. Although King died, his ideas on freedom and equality live on today.

1. What is the main idea of this story?
   a. Martin Luther King, Jr., was a great civil rights leader.
   b. Martin Luther King, Jr., led a march in 1963.
   c. Martin Luther King, Jr., was born in 1929.

2. Where was King born?

   _____

3. What did African Americans have to do on the buses in the 1950s?

   _____

   _____

4. Why did King lead a march in Washington, D.C.?

   _____

5. What happened on April 4, 1968?

   _____

6. What did the civil rights movement do?

   _____

   _____

Read the story. Then, answer the questions.

Elisha Otis

Have you ever ridden on an elevator? Elevators make it much easier for people to get from one floor to another in a tall building. At one time, elevators were not as safe as they are today. Elisha Otis helped change that. Early elevators used ropes that sometimes broke, sending the people riding the elevator to the ground. People could be hurt. Otis made wooden guide rails to go on each side of the elevator. Cables ran through the rails and were connected to a spring that would pull the elevator back up if the cables broke. Otis displayed his invention for the first time at the New York Crystal Palace Exhibition in 1853. His safety elevators were used in buildings as tall as the Eiffel Tower in Paris, France, and the Empire State Building in New York City. Otis died in 1861. His sons, Charles and Norton, continued to sell his design, and many elevators today still have the Otis name on them.

1. What is the main idea of this story?
   a. The Otis family still sells elevators today.
   b. At one time, elevators were unsafe to use.
   c. Elisha Otis found a way to make elevators safe.

2. Why were early elevators dangerous?

   _____

3. What did the spring in Otis's elevators do?

   _____

4. When and where was Otis's elevator displayed for the first time?

   _____

5. What are two buildings that used Otis's elevator design?

   _____

6. What did Otis's sons do after his death?

   _____

   _____

Name _____

Read the story. Then, answer the questions.

Susan B. Anthony

You may know the name Susan B. Anthony from the U.S. dollar coin, but she was famous long before the coin was made. Anthony was a leader who worked for women's rights in the 19th and 20th centuries. She grew up in the Northeast of the United States and was educated at home after a teacher refused to teach her math because she was a girl. Anthony became a teacher and fought for equal wages for women. She attended a special meeting in New York, along with many others, and then began speaking publicly about women's rights. In 1869, Anthony and Elizabeth Cady Stanton formed a group called the National Women's Suffrage Association, which worked to gain women the right to vote. Anthony died in 1906, but American women finally gained the right to vote in 1920, when the Nineteenth Amendment to the U.S. Constitution was passed. Anthony was honored in 1979 with a dollar coin bearing her image.

1. What is the main idea of this story?
   a. Susan B. Anthony could not learn to do math.
   b. Susan B. Anthony worked for women's rights.
   c. A dollar coin honored Susan B. Anthony in 1979.

2. When did Anthony work for women's rights?

   _____

3. Why was Anthony educated at home?

   _____

4. What did Anthony fight for as a teacher?

   _____

5. What did the National Women's Suffrage Association do?

   _____

6. What happened in 1920?

   _____

   _____

Read the story. Then, answer the questions.

Lucy Maud Montgomery

Lucy Maud Montgomery is famous for creating the character of Anne Shirley in her widely read series *Anne of Green Gables*. Montgomery was born in 1874 on Prince Edward Island in Canada. She lived with her grandparents and went to class in a one-room schoolhouse. Her first poem was published when she was only 17 years old. She taught at three island schools and took courses at a university in Nova Scotia. She wrote *Anne of Green Gables* in 1905, but it was not published until 1908. The book became a bestseller, and Montgomery wrote several other books based on the main character. Two films and at least seven TV shows have been made from the *Anne* books. Although Montgomery moved away from Prince Edward Island in 1911, all but one of her books are set there. Many people today still visit the island to see where "Anne Shirley" grew up.

1. What is the main idea of this story?
    a. Lucy Maud Montgomery grew up on Prince Edward Island.
    b. Lucy Maud Montgomery is famous for writing *Anne of Green Gables*.
    c. Lucy Maud Montgomery was a schoolteacher.

2. Who is Anne Shirley?

    _____

3. What was Montgomery's early life like?

    _____

    _____

4. When was Montgomery's first poem published?

    _____

5. How can you tell that *Anne of Green Gables* was a popular book?

    _____

    _____

6. Why do many people visit Prince Edward Island today?

    _____

Read the story. Then, answer the questions.

Roberto Clemente

Roberto Clemente was born in Puerto Rico in 1934. He played baseball in his neighborhood as a child and played for his high school team. He joined a junior national league when he was only 16. He played baseball briefly in Canada before signing to play for the Pittsburgh Pirates in 1954. Clemente served in the U.S. Marine Reserves for several years, which helped him grow physically stronger. He helped the Pirates win two World Series. During the off-season, Clemente often went back to Puerto Rico to help people there. He liked visiting children in hospitals to give them hope that they could get well. After the country of Nicaragua was hit by an earthquake in 1972, Clemente directed relief efforts there. At age 38, he was on his way to deliver supplies to Nicaragua when he died in a plane crash. He was elected to the Baseball Hall of Fame in 1973. He was the first Hispanic player to receive the honor.

1. What is the main idea of this story?
    a. Roberto Clemente was a great baseball player who also helped people.
    b. Roberto Clemente died in a plane crash.
    c. Roberto Clemente was elected to the Baseball Hall of Fame.

2. Where was Clemente born?

    _____

3. Where did Clemente play baseball?

    _____

4. What did Clemente do during the off-season?

    _____

    _____

5. What happened in Nicaragua in 1972?

    _____

6. Why was Clemente flying to Nicaragua?

    _____

Name _____

Read the story. Then, answer the questions.

Lady Bird Johnson

Lady Bird Johnson was born as Claudia Taylor in 1912. She received her nickname after a nurse said that she was as pretty as a ladybird beetle, another name for a ladybug. Lady Bird married Lyndon Baines Johnson in 1934, and together they had two daughters. After President John F. Kennedy's death in 1963, Lyndon Johnson became president of the United States and Lady Bird became First Lady. Most women who serve as First Lady choose a special project to work on. Lady Bird chose to make the highways of the United States more beautiful. She helped get millions of flowers planted, which we can still see today. Lady Bird believed that "where flowers bloom, so does hope." She continued to help make her home state of Texas more beautiful after her husband left office. The Lady Bird Johnson Wildflower Center in Austin, Texas, was opened to help visitors learn about native plants.

1. What is the main idea of this story?
   a. Lady Bird Johnson was born in 1912.
   b. Lady Bird Johnson was married to a president.
   c. Lady Bird Johnson helped make America's highways beautiful.

2. What was Lady Bird Johnson's given name?

   _____

3. How did Lady Bird get her nickname?

   _____

   _____

4. How did Lady Bird become the First Lady?

   _____

   _____

5. What does the Wildflower Center in Austin, Texas, do?

   _____

6. What did Lady Bird accomplish as First Lady?

   _____

Name _____

Read the story. Then, answer the questions.

James Naismith

Have you ever played basketball with your friends? You dribble the ball, run down the court, and shoot it through a hoop. The modern game of basketball was invented by James Naismith, a Canadian gym teacher, in 1891. Naismith wanted a game that would not take up too much room and that could be played indoors. He nailed peach baskets at both ends of the gym and sorted his players into two teams of nine each. The players passed a ball to each other and threw it into the basket when they reached the end of the court. Eventually, players started to bounce the ball instead of just tossing it to each other. This bouncing motion became known as dribbling. Basketball soon caught on among both men's and women's teams. It became an official Olympic sport in 1936, and Naismith was invited to watch. Naismith died in 1939, but his sport lives on. Over 300 million people around the world play basketball today.

1. What is the main idea of this story?
   a. James Naismith's sport lives on today.
   b. James Naismith was a gym teacher.
   c. James Naismith invented the sport of basketball.

2. What are three things players do in basketball?

   _____

   _____

3. What kind of game did Naismith want to invent?

   _____

   _____

4. What did the first basketball hoops look like?

   _____

5. In the early days of the sport, what did basketball players do before they learned to dribble?

   _____

6. How can you tell that basketball is still popular today?

   _____

Name _____

Read the story. Then, answer the questions.

Babe Didrikson Zaharias

Babe Didrikson Zaharias was an outstanding sportswoman. She played golf, basketball, and baseball and also ran track. Zaharias grew up playing sports with her six brothers and sisters in Port Arthur, Texas. She played basketball with a company team when she worked as a secretary. She joined the U.S. Olympic team and won medals in three track-and-field events at the 1932 Olympics in Los Angeles. Zaharias began playing golf in 1935, and in 1938 she became the first woman to play in a PGA (Professional Golf Association) game. She became famous for her playing, and in 1950 she helped form the LPGA (Ladies Professional Golf Association). This group continues to hold golf matches for female golfers today. Zaharias died in 1956, but she was named to the U.S. Olympic Hall of Fame in 1983. People can learn more about Zaharias's life by visiting a museum in her honor in Beaumont, Texas.

1. What is the main idea of this story?
    a. Babe Didrikson Zaharias grew up in Texas.
    b. Babe Didrikson Zaharias was good at many sports.
    c. Babe Didrikson Zaharias died in 1956.

2. Which sports did Zaharias play?

    _____

3. What happened to Zaharias at the 1932 Olympics?

    _____

4. What did Zaharias do in 1938?

    _____

5. What honor did Zaharias receive in 1983?

    _____

6. What does the LPGA do today?

    _____

    _____

Name _____

Read the story. Then, answer the questions.

Edward R. Murrow

Edward R. Murrow was an American journalist who became famous during the Second World War. He was born in 1908 in North Carolina. After college, Murrow began working for a radio station. People all over America listened to his live broadcasts from the bombing of London, England, in September 1939, known as the Blitz. Before Murrow's reports, people in the United States could only learn about the war through newsreels in movie theaters or articles in newspapers. Now, they could listen to Murrow on their radios at home. Murrow was very brave to risk his life so that Americans could learn about the war in London. After the war ended, Murrow continued to work as a reporter in radio and then in television. On TV, he became known for interviewing, or asking questions of, famous people. Other newscasters followed in Murrow's footsteps, and today we still look forward to hearing from reporters in other countries and listening in on their chats with famous people.

1. What is the main idea of this story?
    a. Edward R. Murrow was a brave American journalist.
    b. Edward R. Murrow talked to many famous people.
    c. Edward R. Murrow worked in London.

2. What type of company did Murrow work for?

    _____

3. What was special about Murrow's broadcasts in 1939?

    _____

4. How did people learn about the war before Murrow's work?

    _____

    _____

5. What did Murrow do after the war ended?

    _____

6. How did Murrow change the way journalists work?

    _____

    _____

 CD-104305 • © Carson-Dellosa

Name _____

Read the story. Then, answer the questions.

Thomas Edison

Without Thomas Alva Edison, we might all be sitting around in the dark! Although people before Edison worked on designs for the lightbulb, he is credited with creating the modern electric light. Edison was born in 1847. He worked as a telegraph operator. Edison liked working on the night shift so that he could have plenty of time to read and conduct experiments during the day. He invented the phonograph, or record player, in 1877. Edison built his own lab at Menlo Park, New Jersey, where he could continue to work on his inventions. The lab covered the space of two city blocks. Edison showed his lightbulb to the public in 1879. At this time, most people used candles to light their homes. The candles sometimes caused house fires. By 1887, over 100 power plants were sending electricity to customers. Edison registered over 1,000 patents, or designs, for different inventions. It is no wonder that a newspaper called him the Wizard of Menlo Park!

1. What is the main idea of this story?
    a. Thomas Edison built his own lab.
    b. Thomas Edison was a successful American inventor.
    c. Thomas Edison worked on the night shift.

2. What are two of Edison's inventions?

    _____

3. Why did Edison like working on the night shift?

    _____

    _____

4. How large was Edison's lab at Menlo Park?

    _____

5. How many different inventions did Edison create?

    _____

6. How did the lightbulb change people's lives?

    _____

    _____

Read the story. Then, answer the questions.

Harriet Tubman

Harriet Tubman was a brave woman. Tubman grew up as a slave in Maryland but escaped north to Philadelphia, Pennsylvania, as an adult. She returned to Maryland to help rescue her family and returned again and again to help other slaves. She guided them to safe houses along a network known as the Underground Railroad. People who helped slaves move to safety were called "conductors," after the people who controlled trains on railroads. In 1861, the United States began fighting the Civil War, which was partly a struggle between northern and southern states over whether people should be allowed to own slaves. In 1863, President Abraham Lincoln signed a law stating that slavery was no longer allowed in the United States. With the law on her side, Tubman continued to help people who were treated unfairly until her death in 1913.

1. What is the main idea of this story?
    a. Harriet Tubman was a former slave.
    b. Harriet Tubman lived in Maryland.
    c. Harriet Tubman helped people on the Underground Railroad.

2. What did people in Tubman's time believe about slavery?

    _____

    _____

3. Why did Tubman return to Maryland?

    _____

4. What was the Underground Railroad?

    _____

5. What did conductors on the Underground Railroad do?

    _____

6. What was the Civil War?

    _____

    _____

Name _____

Read the story. Then, answer the questions.

Titanic

In the spring of 1912, a luxury ship called the *Titanic* set off from England on its first journey. The *Titanic* was headed for New York City, but on the night of April 14, its journey was cut short. Around midnight, the ship hit an iceberg, and in less than three hours the ship had sunk. Although over 700 people survived the disaster, more than 1,500 lives were lost in the icy waters of the Atlantic. Because of the way the *Titanic* was built, everyone thought it was impossible for the ship to sink. This certainty led to several of the causes of the disaster. We now know that the captain had ignored warnings of ice and pushed the *Titanic* too fast through dangerous waters. We also know that there were not enough lifeboats for everyone on board. Because of the *Titanic* disaster, new rules were set. Now people know that every ship can sink and so there must be a space in a lifeboat for every person on a ship.

1. What is the main idea of this story?
   a. The *Titanic* was unsinkable.
   b. The sinking of the *Titanic* was a huge disaster.
   c. A ship called the *Titanic* left England in 1912.

2. How was the *Titanic*'s journey cut short?

   _____

3. Why did everyone think that it was impossible for the *Titanic* to sink?

   _____

4. What does the story say led to several causes of the disaster?

   _____

5. What could the captain have done to help avoid this disaster?

   _____

6. What might have been different if the *Titanic* had had enough lifeboats for everyone?

   _____

   _____

Read the story. Then, answer the questions.

Elijah McCoy

You may have heard something referred to as "the real McCoy." This expression means "the real thing" instead of a copy. Some people think that "the real McCoy" was Elijah McCoy, who was born in Canada in 1843. His parents were former slaves who escaped from Kentucky to Canada. At the time, slavery was illegal in Canada but not in the United States. McCoy traveled to Scotland when he was 16 to learn how to design, build, and repair machines. After the Civil War ended, he moved to Michigan, where he worked on the railroad. He had to pour oil into the engine whenever the train stopped. McCoy worked on inventions at his home machine shop, where he came up with the idea for a better way to carry oil into train engines. His invention helped trains run more smoothly. Railroad workers would ask for "the real McCoy" because it was better than other machines like it.

1. What is the main idea of this story?
    a. Elijah McCoy created a tool to keep train engines running.
    b. Elijah McCoy was "the real McCoy" that the saying refers to.
    c. Elijah McCoy spent several years in Scotland.

2. What does the phrase "the real McCoy" mean?

    _____

3. Why did McCoy's parents move to Canada?

    _____

    _____

4. Why did McCoy travel to Scotland?

    _____

5. What did McCoy's invention do?

    _____

6. Why did workers ask for "the real McCoy"?

    _____

    _____

Read the story. Then, answer the questions.

Louisa May Alcott

For nearly 150 years, children have grown up reading about Meg, Jo, Beth, and Amy, in Louisa May Alcott's famous book *Little Women*. Alcott grew up with three sisters in Massachusetts. Like the girls in the book, Alcott and her sisters liked to put on plays for their friends. Her family was very poor, and Alcott helped them by working as a maid, a teacher, a nurse, and finally a writer. Her books about the March family, beginning with *Little Women*, were widely read during her lifetime. The main character, Jo, based on Alcott herself, works as a writer until she marries and has a family. Alcott continued to write until her death in 1888. She also spoke out for women's rights and against slavery. Today, people can visit Orchard House, the home where Alcott grew up and where *Little Women* is set.

1. What is the main idea of this story?
    a. Louisa May Alcott was very poor as a child.
    b. Louisa May Alcott had three sisters.
    c. Louisa May Alcott based her books on her own life.

2. How was Alcott's family like the March family?

   _____

   _____

3. How did Alcott help her family?

   _____

   _____

4. Who was the character of Jo based on?

   _____

5. What was Alcott known for besides writing?

   _____

6. How was Alcott different from the character Jo in *Little Women*?

   _____

   _____

Name _____

Read the story. Then, answer the questions.

Wayne Gretzky

Wayne Gretzky is called "The Great One" by fans of Canadian hockey. He scored over 1,000 goals during his career. Gretzky was born in Brantford, Ontario, and learned to ice-skate on his family's farm when he was three. Gretzky's father taught him and his three brothers to play hockey on a frozen pond in the backyard. When Gretzky was six, he joined a league of 10-year-olds and began playing on a team. In the summer, he played baseball and lacrosse. He started playing for a professional hockey team, the Indianapolis Racers, when he was 17. He played for the Edmonton Oilers in Canada for nine years, during which they won hockey's Stanley Cup four times. He also played for several U.S. teams. Gretzky retired from the sport in 1999 and was voted into the Hockey Hall of Fame. Both his hometown of Brantford and his adopted city of Edmonton named streets after Gretzky to honor him.

1. What is the main idea of this story?
    a. Wayne Gretzky was a great hockey player.
    b. Wayne Gretzky had three brothers.
    c. Wayne Gretzky played hockey in the United States and Canada.

2. Why is Gretzky called "The Great One" by Canadian hockey fans?

    _____

3. Where did Gretzky first play hockey?

    _____

4. What other sports did Gretzky play?

    _____

5. How did Gretzky help the Edmonton Oilers?

    _____

6. What are three honors that Gretzky received?

    _____

    _____

Name _____

Read the story. Then, answer the questions.

Computers

Have you ever used a computer at school, at the library, or at home? Today's computers can fit on a desktop or in your lap. Computers of the past took up a whole room! One of the first computers was called the ENIAC, which stood for Electronic Numerical Integrator and Calculator. It took up 1,800 square feet (about 167 square meters), weighed nearly 50 tons, and cost $500,000. The ENIAC took three years to build and was designed for the U.S. Army. It required a team of six people to program it, or tell it what to do. The ENIAC was used from 1947 to 1955. In contrast, a personal computer today can weigh as little as two pounds (about one kilogram) and can be operated by one person at a time. The builders of the ENIAC may never have believed students could do their homework on a computer.

1. What is the main idea of this story?
    a. The ENIAC was an early computer.
    b. Computers of the past were very different from ones today.
    c. Students can do their homework on computers.

2. What does *ENIAC* stand for?

    _____

3. How large was ENIAC?

    _____

4. What does the word *program* mean in this story?
    a. build a computer
    b. require six people to use
    c. tell a computer what to do

5. When was the ENIAC used?

    _____

6. How are computers today different from those of the past?

    _____

    _____

Name _____

Read the story. Then, answer the questions.

Food Webs

A food web is a drawing that shows how different living things are connected. On the web drawing, it shows which animals at the top eat the animals directly below them, and so on until the bottom of the web. For example, a food web might start at the bottom with plants like grass and nuts, which do not eat other living things. Above these plants might be small animals such as mice and insects. Larger animals like owls and snakes eat the smaller animals. A food web can tell you what might happen if different plants or animals disappear from an ecosystem, or the surroundings in which all of these things live. In the food web described above, if something happened to the grass, then the mice and insects would not have much food. This would affect the owls and snakes, which would also not have enough food. Soon, there would be fewer of every animal. This is why it is important to protect all living things in an ecosystem, not just the largest ones.

1. What is the main idea of this story?
    a. Food webs show how all living things are connected.
    b. Owls and snakes are the most important animals.
    c. Only the animals at the top should be protected.

2. What is a food web?

   _____

3. What is at the bottom of a food web?

   _____

4. What might happen if the insects in a food web were gone?

   _____

5. What is an *ecosystem*?
    a. a food web for very large animals
    b. the surroundings where a group of plants and animals live
    c. a place that grows only grass and nuts

6. Why is it important to protect all living things in an ecosystem?

   _____

   _____

Name _____

Read the story. Then, answer the questions.

Science Experiments

Scientists learn about the world by conducting experiments. They take careful notes on the supplies they use and the results they find. They share their findings with others, which leads to everyone learning a little more. You can do experiments too! The library has many books with safe experiments for students. You might work with balloons, water, or baking soda. You might learn about how light travels or why marbles roll down a ramp. Ask an adult to help you set up your experiment and to watch to make sure you are being safe. Be sure to wash your hands afterward and clean up the area. Take good notes on your work. You may be able to change just one thing the next time to get a completely different result. Most of all, do not worry if your results are different than you expected. Some of the greatest scientific discoveries were made by mistake!

1. What is the main idea of this story?
   a. Children can do experiments too, as long as they are safe.
   b. Scientists often make mistakes that lead to great discoveries.
   c. You should always take good notes when conducting an experiment.

2. What do scientists take notes on?

   _____

3. What happens when scientists share their findings with others?

   _____

4. Where can you find information about safe experiments?

   _____

5. Why should you ask an adult to help?

   _____

6. Should you worry if you get different results? Why or why not?

   _____

   _____

Read the story. Then, answer the questions.

Magnets

A magnet is any object with a magnetic field. This means that it pulls things made of iron, steel, or nickel toward it. If you set a paper clip next to a magnet on a table, the paper clip will move toward the magnet. Every magnet has what is called a north pole and a south pole. The north pole of one magnet will stick to the south pole of another magnet. If you try to push the south poles of two magnets together, they will spring apart. Earth has magnetic poles too. Earth is a big magnet! Earth's magnetic poles are not actual places. They are areas of Earth's magnetic field with a certain property. Although Earth's magnetic poles are different than the poles like the one where polar bears live, its magnetic poles are near these poles. The north pole of a magnet will always try to point toward Earth's north magnetic pole. A piece of camping equipment called a compass works by having a magnetized needle that points to Earth's magnetic north pole. So, if you get lost, you could set the compass on a flat surface and wait for the needle to point north.

1. What is the main idea of this story?
    a. If you get lost in the woods, start walking north.
    b. Compasses work by pointing to the north.
    c. Magnets are objects that have magnetic fields.

2. What happens if you put a paper clip next to a magnet?

    _____

3. How is Earth like a magnet?

    _____

4. What happens if you push a north pole and a south pole together?

    _____

5. What happens if you push two south poles together?

    _____

6. How does a compass work?

    _____

    _____

Read the story. Then, answer the questions.

Solid, Liquid, Gas

All matter on Earth exists in one of three states: solid, liquid, or gas. Solids, such as boxes or books, have a certain shape that is hard to change. Liquids, such as lemonade or orange juice, take the shape of the bottle or cup they are in. Gases, such as the air you breathe, spread out to fill the space they are in. It is easy to change water from one state to another. The water that you drink is a liquid. When water is heated, such as in a pot on the stove, it becomes a gas. This gas is known as steam, or vapor. Steam is used in an iron to make clothes smooth. It also can be used in a large machine to make electricity. When water is frozen, such as in a tray in the freezer, it turns into ice. Ice is used to cool down drinks or to help a hurt part of the body heal.

1. What is the main idea of this story?
    a. Steam is heated water.
    b. All matter exists as a solid, liquid, or gas.
    c. Ice cubes make water taste better.

2. What are two examples of solids?

    _____

3. What are two examples of liquids?

    _____

4. What are two examples of gases?

    _____

5. What do you call water in the three states of matter?

    _____

6. How are solids, liquids, and gases different from one another?

    _____

    _____

    _____

Name _____

Read the story. Then, answer the questions.

Tornadoes

A tornado is a funnel cloud that forms over land. It is created when warm air meets cold air, making a thunderstorm. Tornadoes can be very dangerous to both people and things. They can leave a trail of damage one mile (1.6 km) wide and 50 miles (80 km) long. The wind speed can reach over 300 miles (480 km) per hour. People often have little warning of a tornado, but certain parts of the United States have tornadoes more frequently than other parts. The area called "Tornado Alley" covers parts of Texas, Oklahoma, Kansas, Nebraska, Iowa, and South Dakota. Tornadoes are more likely to form in the spring and summer. If the weather reporter says that a tornado has been spotted in your area, stay inside. Go to the lowest level of your home, keep as many walls as possible between you and the outside, and keep the windows closed. Do not leave until you hear that the tornado has passed.

1. What is the main idea of this story?
    a. Tornadoes are formed during thunderstorms.
    b. Tornado Alley is an area where many storms occur.
    c. Tornadoes are dangerous to people and buildings.

2. What is a tornado?

    _____

    _____

3. How far can the damage from a tornado reach?

    _____

4. What are three states that are found in Tornado Alley?

    _____

5. When are tornadoes more likely to form?

    _____

6. What should you do if a tornado is spotted in your area?

    _____

    _____

Read the story. Then, answer the questions.

Floods

Rain is good for people and plants, but when it rains too much, people may be in danger. A flash flood occurs when a lot of rain falls very quickly, filling up the streets faster than the water can drain away. It is very dangerous to drive in a flash flood, because your car may be swept away. If you live in an area where flooding is likely, listen to the radio or television when it starts to rain. Be ready to leave your home if the newscaster tells you to move to a higher location. Before you leave, turn off all electrical equipment. Move important items to a higher floor, if possible. If you leave on foot, do not walk through moving water. Do not drive through standing water unless it is less than six inches (15.24 cm) deep. After a flood, listen to news reports to find out when you can return home and when the water from your tap will be safe to drink.

1. What is the main idea of this story?
    a. Flash floods can be dangerous and happen suddenly.
    b. Never drive through a flooded area.
    c. Take important items with you when you leave your home.

2. What happens during a flash flood?

    _____

3. What could happen to a car in a flash flood?

    _____

4. When should you leave your home?

    _____

5. What should you do before leaving your home?

    _____

    _____

6. What should you do after a flood?

    _____

    _____

Name _____

Read the story. Then, answer the questions.

Glaciers

A glacier is a large, thick mass of ice. It forms when snow hardens into ice over a long period of time. It might not look like it, but glaciers can move. They usually move very slowly, but if a lot of the ice melts at once, the glacier may surge forward, or move suddenly over a long distance. Most glaciers are found in Antarctica, the continent at the South Pole, or in Greenland, which is near the North Pole. Areas with glaciers receive a lot of snowfall in the winter and have cool summers. Most glaciers are located in the mountains, where few people live, but occasionally they can cause flooding in cities and towns. Falling ice from glaciers may block the path of people hiking on a trail farther down on the mountain. Icebergs, or large floating pieces of ice, may break off from glaciers and cause problems for ships at sea.

1. What is the main idea of this story?
    a. Icebergs can be dangerous to ships.
    b. Glaciers are large masses of ice found mainly in the mountains.
    c. People usually live far from glaciers.

2. How does a glacier form?

   _____

3. What does the word *surge* mean in this story?
    a. move forward suddenly
    b. freeze into ice
    c. break off from an iceberg

4. Where are most glaciers found?

   _____

5. What is the weather like where glaciers are found?

   _____

6. How can glaciers be dangerous?

   _____

   _____

   _____

Name _____

Read the story. Then, answer the questions.

Health and Fitness

Health and fitness are very important for young people. If you start good habits now, you have a better chance of being a healthy adult later. You may go to gym class several times a week, but you should also try to stay fit outside of school. You and your family can make healthy choices together. You can choose fresh fruit for dessert instead of cake. Offer to help make dinner one night and surprise your family by preparing a delicious salad. You can go for a walk together after dinner instead of watching television. Exercising can help wake up your brain so that you can do a good job on your homework. Making healthy choices may seem hard now, but after a while it will feel good.

1. What is the main idea of this story?
   a. Going to gym class is fun.
   b. Making healthy choices is too hard.
   c. Health and fitness are important for you and your family.

2. What might happen if you start good habits now?

   _____

   _____

3. Where should you try to stay fit?

   _____

4. What is a better choice than cake for dessert?

   _____

5. What can you do instead of watching TV after dinner?

   _____

6. How does exercise affect your brain?

   _____

   _____

Name _____

Read the story. Then, answer the questions.

Reptiles and Amphibians

You may think that lizards and frogs are in the same family, but they are actually quite different. Lizards, snakes, turtles, and crocodiles are all reptiles. Frogs, toads, and salamanders are amphibians. Both amphibians and reptiles are cold-blooded, which means the warmth of their bodies depends on their surroundings. Most animals in both categories lay eggs instead of giving birth to their young. Reptiles lay hard-shelled eggs in nests, but amphibians lay soft-shelled eggs underwater. When reptiles hatch, they look like tiny adults. Amphibian babies like tadpoles, or baby frogs, have to live underwater until they are older. Adult amphibians spend part of their time in the water and part on land. Reptiles feel dry and scaly to the touch. Amphibians feel moist and sticky. Because amphibians can live both in water and on land, they are more at risk for becoming sick from pollution. It is important to keep ponds and lakes clean so that the animals that live there will be safe.

1. What is the main idea of this story?
   a. There are important differences between reptiles and amphibians.
   b. Reptiles are the same as amphibians.
   c. Frogs and lizards belong to different families.

2. What are three animals that are reptiles?

   _____

3. What are three animals that are amphibians?

   _____

4. How are amphibians and reptiles similar?

   _____

5. Why is it important to keep ponds and lakes clean?

   _____

6. What are three differences between reptiles and amphibians?

   _____

   _____

Name _____

Read the story. Then, answer the questions.

Dolphins and Sharks

Both dolphins and sharks have fins and live in the ocean, but there are many differences between them. Dolphins are mammals, and sharks are fish. Dolphins have smooth, rubbery skin. Like other mammals, they have hair. Dolphins are born with a few whiskers on their chins, though the whiskers may fall out after birth. Shark skin is covered in tough scales that feel like sandpaper and look like tiny teeth. Baby dolphins stay with their mothers for about three years to learn how to hunt. Baby sharks can start hunting by themselves soon after birth. Dolphins have lungs, so they must come to the surface of the water to breathe. A dolphin shoots air through a blowhole on top of its head like a whale. Sharks breathe through gills, so they can stay underwater much longer. People and dolphins may not look much alike, but they have more in common than dolphins and sharks!

1. What is the main idea of this story?
   a. People and dolphins have nothing in common.
   b. Dolphins and sharks look alike but are very different.
   c. Whales and dolphins both have blowholes.

2. How is dolphin skin different from shark skin?

   _____

   _____

3. Why do baby dolphins stay with their mothers after birth?

   _____

4. Why must dolphins come to the surface of the water?

   _____

5. Why can sharks stay underwater for a long time?

   _____

6. What has more in common with dolphins than sharks do?

   _____

   _____

Name _____

Read the story. Then, answer the questions.

Turtles and Tortoises

Turtles and tortoises look very similar, and they are both reptiles. They both have shells that they can pull their heads and legs into in case of danger. They both lay eggs, have scales, and are cold-blooded. However, there are some differences between them. Turtles live in or near the water and can hold their breath for a long period of time while they swim. Tortoises live on land, often in areas that are hot and dry. Turtles have flippers or webbed feet that help them swim. Tortoises have hard, scaly feet that are good for walking on rocks and hard ground. They may have claws to help them dig burrows for resting. Turtles eat insects and fish as well as plants, but tortoises eat mostly plants, such as cactus. If you find an animal that looks like a turtle in your backyard, it is most likely a tortoise.

1. What is the main idea of this story?
    a. Reptiles have scales and lay eggs.
    b. Tortoises like to eat lettuce.
    c. Turtles and tortoises are both reptiles but have some differences.

2. What do turtles and tortoises do in case of danger?

    _____

3. Where do turtles and tortoises live?

    _____

4. How does a turtle's body help it live in the water?

    _____

5. How do a tortoise's feet help it live on land?

    _____

    _____

6. Why would a turtle in your backyard really be a tortoise?

    _____

    _____

    _____

CD-104305 • © Carson-Dellosa

Name _____

Read the story. Then, answer the questions.

Sea Urchins

Sea urchins look like pincushions that live under the sea. They have long, thin spines that stick out all over their bodies. Most sea urchins have spines that are about 0.39 to 1.18 inches (1 to 3 cm) long. Sea urchins are found in oceans all over the world. They can be many colors, from green to brown to red. Their bodies are about 4 inches (10 cm) across. They eat dead fish, seaweed, and very tiny plants called algae. Their spines help them trap food. They also use their five tiny teeth to pull plants off rocks. Hundreds of tiny tubes used as feet help them move along the seafloor. Many creatures, including sea otters, crabs, and eels, like to eat sea urchins.

1. What is the main idea of this story?
   a. Sea urchins are interesting animals that live in the ocean.
   b. Sea urchins taste salty and creamy.
   c. Sea urchins look like pincushions.

2. What do sea urchins' spines look like?

   _____

3. What do sea urchins eat?

   _____

4. How do sea urchins get food?

   _____

   _____

5. How do sea urchins move?

   _____

6. Which creatures like to eat sea urchins?

   _____

   _____

Read the story. Then, answer the questions.

Silkworms

Silk is a soft, smooth type of cloth that is used for clothing, bedding, and wall hangings. It comes from silkworm cocoons, which are spun into thread that is then made into cloth. It takes about 3,000 cocoons to make one pound (about 0.5 kg) of silk. Silkworms become moths as adults. Like most insects, silkworms go through four stages. The moth lays its eggs on a mulberry leaf. After a silkworm hatches into a caterpillar, it munches on leaves until it grows to the length of a human finger. After about a month of eating and growing, the worm spins a cocoon of silk around itself. Spinning the cocoon takes about three days. Inside the cocoon, the silkworm changes shape and becomes a pupa. After about three weeks, the pupa turns into a moth. The moth comes out of the cocoon and starts the cycle all over again.

1. What is the main idea of this story?
    a. Silkworm cocoons are spun into thread.
    b. Silkworms turn into moths as adults.
    c. Silkworms go through four stages and help make silk.

2. What is silk used for?

    _____

3. What are the stages of a silkworm's life?

    _____

4. What do silkworms eat?

    _____

5. How long does it take to spin a cocoon?
    a. 3,000 days
    b. about three days
    c. about three weeks

6. What happens to the silkworm inside the cocoon?

    _____

    _____

Name _____

Read the story. Then, answer the questions.

The Olympic Games

In the Olympic Games, people from all over the world gather together to compete in different sports. The original Olympics were held in Greece around 776 BCE. Young men came together every four years to run races of different lengths. Those who won were given wreaths of olive branches. The modern Olympics were first held in 1896 in Greece. In 1996, people decided that the summer and winter Olympic Games should be held in different years. This means that every two years, thousands of people representing over 200 countries come together to compete in either summer or winter sports. Today's winners receive gold, silver, or bronze medals and compete in hundreds of different events. The Olympics give the host countries a chance to show their culture both to the people who come there and to people who watch on TV. The sports may be different than the original Olympics, but the spirit of goodwill and good sportsmanship is still the same.

1. What is the main idea of this story?
   a. The Olympics are held every four years.
   b. People come to the Olympics to compete in different sports.
   c. Good sportsmanship is very important at the Olympics.

2. When and where were the first Olympics held?

   _____

3. What did winners receive at the early Olympics?

   _____

4. How did the Olympics change in 1996?

   _____

   _____

5. What do Olympic winners receive today?

   _____

6. How do the Olympics help people learn about different cultures?

   _____

   _____

Read the story. Then, answer the questions.

Flags of the World

A flag tells something special about an area or a group. For example, the U.S. flag has 13 red and white stripes for the first 13 states, and 50 stars on a blue field for the current 50 states. The Canadian flag has a red maple leaf on white between two bands of red. The maple leaf stands for the nature found in Canada. Canadian provinces and U.S. states also have their own flags. The state flag of Texas has a large white star on blue on the left and two bands of red and white on the right. Because of the flag's single star, Texas is called the Lone Star State. The flag of the Canadian province of New Brunswick has a gold lion on a red field above a sailing ship. The lion stands for ties to Brunswick, Germany, and the British king. The ship represents the shipping industry. The flag of the United Nations, a group of countries that works for world peace, shows a globe surrounded by olive leaves.

1. What is the main idea of this story?
   a. Flags tell something special about a country or group.
   b. Some flags have maple leaves or lions on them.
   c. Many flags are red, white, or blue.

2. What does the U.S. flag look like?

   _____

   _____

3. What does the Canadian flag look like?

   _____

4. Why is Texas called the Lone Star State?

   _____

5. What does the word *field* mean in this story?
   a. an area of grass
   b. a large area of a single color
   c. an area of study

6. What does the flag of the United Nations have on it?

   _____

Read the story. Then, answer the questions.

The Continents

Earth is divided into seven large areas of land called continents. The seven continents are Asia, Africa, Australia, Europe, Antarctica, North America, and South America. Each continent is separated from the others by a feature such as an ocean or a mountain range. Continents may be divided into many different countries, states, or provinces. People live on six of the seven continents. The continent of Antarctica is at the South Pole, where the weather is too cold for people to live. Some scientists study in Antarctica at special stations, but many stay there for only part of the year. The largest continent is Asia, which covers over 17,000,000 square miles (44,000,000 square km). The smallest is Australia, which covers nearly 3,000,000 square miles (7,700,000 square km). Asia also has the most people, with a population of over three billion. That accounts for about half the world's people!

1. What is the main idea of this story?
   a. More people live in Asia than on any other continent.
   b. It is hard for people to live in Antarctica.
   c. Continents are large areas of land on Earth.

2. List the seven continents.

   _____

   _____

3. What separates continents from each other?

   _____

4. What is a *station* in the story?
   a. a place where scientists study
   b. an area of the classroom
   c. a television channel

5. About how much bigger is Asia than Australia?

   _____

6. Why do you think that so many people live in Asia?

   _____

Name _____

Read the story. Then, answer the questions.

Community Helpers

A community is a group of people who live in the same area or have the same interests. Communities need helpers to make them work. Some important community helpers are police officers and firefighters. Police officers make sure everyone is following the rules of the community to keep people safe. Firefighters put out fires and educate people about fire safety. Other community helpers are people who work for the city, such as garbage collectors and park rangers. Garbage collectors drive down city streets to pick up trash that people have put in bags or cans at the curb. Park rangers make sure city parks are clean and safe so that people can play or have picnics in them. Another important helper in the community is a librarian. The librarian makes sure there are lots of good books available for everyone in the community to read. The next time you see a community helper, say "Thank you!"

1. What is the main idea of this story?
   a. A community needs a lot of people to make it work.
   b. Police officers and firefighters are community helpers.
   c. People like to have picnics in city parks.

2. What do police officers do in a community?

   _____

   _____

3. What do firefighters do in a community?

   _____

4. How do garbage collectors help the community?

   _____

5. Why does a community need park rangers?

   _____

6. Why should you say "Thank you!" to a community helper?

   _____

   _____

Name _____

Read the story. Then, answer the questions.

World Holidays

You and your family may celebrate several special days a year. People in different countries recognize different holidays. Many people in China have a Lantern Festival to celebrate the new year. They light special lamps and hold colorful parades through the streets. In Scotland, some people celebrate Burns Night, in honor of the Scottish poet Robert Burns. Families or clubs gather together for a special meal and a reading of Burns's poetry on his birthday. While people in the United States celebrate their independence on Independence Day, people in Canada celebrate Canada Day. On July 1, 1867, the government of Canada was created. On both Canada Day and Independence Day, people have community parades and picnics. People in some parts of Germany celebrate Oktoberfest to mark the harvest. They eat traditional German foods like sausage and potato salad. People who went to other countries carried their traditions to their new homes, so many places outside of those countries celebrate the same holidays.

1. What is the main idea of this story?
   a. Burns Night is a special holiday in Scotland.
   b. People around the world celebrate different holidays.
   c. Oktoberfest takes place in many cities.

2. What is a *lantern* in the story?
   a. a type of food eaten in China
   b. a special holiday
   c. a type of lamp

3. How do people in Scotland honor Robert Burns?

   _____

4. How are Independence Day and Canada Day celebrations alike?

   _____

5. What does Oktoberfest represent?

   _____

6. Why might someone take their traditions to a new country?

   _____

Read the story. Then, answer the questions.

The Right to Vote

Some people think that the most important right of a citizen of a country is the right to vote. Only adults over age 18 are allowed to vote in Canada and the United States. Until the 1970s, only people over 21 could vote! People today can vote for a number of government offices, including the president, vice president, and mayor. They may also vote on laws that affect their city, such as rules about how to use areas of land or what kinds of businesses can be on a given street. In many countries, elections use a secret ballot. This means that no one except the person voting can see who they are voting for. Without a secret ballot, someone might tell you to vote for a certain leader. Each person is allowed to vote only once. This means that everyone gets an equal say in which leaders get elected to office.

1. What is the main idea of this story?
    a. Voting helps people elect their government.
    b. Only adults over 18 can vote.
    c. Everyone has an equal say in government.

2. How did the voting laws change in the 1970s?

    _____

3. Which government offices can people vote for?

    _____

4. What kinds of laws can people vote on?

    _____

5. What is a *secret ballot*?
    a. a kind of dancing
    b. a vote that no one else can see
    c. a type of song

6. Why is each person only allowed to vote once?

    _____

    _____

Name _____

Read the story. Then, answer the questions.

City Government

The president and prime minister are important national leaders, but there are also important leaders in your city. Many cities have a mayor, who is responsible for attending events like the opening of a new library or a parade. The mayor often works with a group of people known as a city council. These people come from areas all over the city. They work together to come up with solutions that will work for all citizens. A city may also have a manager, who makes sure that city services are running smoothly day to day. The city manager also creates a budget to show how the city should spend its money. Other members of the city government include the chief of police and the fire chief. These people lead the police and fire departments. They make the rules that all of their employees must follow. A city needs many workers to make a better life for all of its citizens.

1. What is the main idea of this story?
    a. The president is an important leader.
    b. The leader of the police is called a chief.
    c. City government includes many different workers.

2. What does a mayor do?

   _____

3. Where do members of a city council come from?

   _____

4. What does a city manager do?

   _____

   _____

5. What is a *budget*?
    a. a report that tells how the city should spend its money
    b. a city manager
    c. a person who leads the fire department

6. Why does a city need many workers?

   _____

Read the story. Then, answer the questions.

Planning a City

What do the streets in your city look like? Some cities have streets that are very straight and organized. It is easy to get from one point in the city to another. Other cities have streets that seem to go nowhere. It may be difficult to give directions to your home. When a group of people move to a place and start setting up the streets, they may use something called a grid system. One example of this is found in the city of Philadelphia, Pennsylvania, which is divided into four sections around a central square. The map was laid out by William Penn in 1682. The grid included wide streets that were easy for people to walk down. Penn left London, England, after a fire destroyed most of the city. London had a maze of narrow streets that were hard to move around safely. Penn wanted to make sure people could get around the city easily and safely. Many other cities followed Penn's ideas when setting up their street systems.

1. What is the main idea of this story?
    a. William Penn drew the first grid system.
    b. Planning a city is important for safety.
    c. Some streets are straight and organized.

2. What is one good thing about having straight streets?

    _____

3. What is a grid system?
    a. a way of arranging straight streets in a city
    b. a maze of narrow streets
    c. a famous fire in London

4. What is one good thing about having wide streets?

    _____

5. Why did Penn leave London?

    _____

6. How are Philadelphia's streets different from London's?

    _____

    _____

Read the story. Then, answer the questions.

Musical Cultures

People from different cultures celebrate different holidays and eat different kinds of food. They also have different musical cultures. The United States has many musical traditions. People in New Orleans, Louisiana, in the southern part of the United States, are known for a style of music called jazz. This music has strong rhythms and allows people to play freely. People from a region of the eastern United States called Appalachia play folk music with fiddles and banjos. Much of this music is based on the songs and dance tunes of the British Isles. Countries that border each other have music styles from the people who cross from one country to the other. Some styles from Mexico are *banda* and *cumbia*. Some Canadian styles of music are based on French songs and use accordions and guitars. Because of the radio and television, people all over the world can hear music of other cultures and create new musical traditions of their own.

1. What is the main idea of this story?
   a. Different cultures have different holidays and food.
   b. Some Canadian music is based on French songs.
   c. People have different musical cultures.

2. What is jazz?

   _____

   _____

3. What is one type of music that has fiddles and banjos?

   _____

4. What are some styles of music from Mexico?

   _____

5. What is some Canadian music based on?

   _____

6. How do radio and television affect musical cultures?

   _____

   _____

Name _____

Read the story. Then, answer the questions.

Cleaning Up Earth

There are many cities to live in, but we have only one Earth. It is important to take care of our planet because we cannot move to a new one. You may have heard the phrase "Reduce, reuse, recycle." Putting these words into action will help keep Earth clean. First, try to *reduce* the amount of waste you produce. You can cook with fresh fruits and vegetables instead of packaged foods. Second, *reuse* things when you can. You can make a bird feeder from a milk carton that would otherwise go in the trash. You can also donate your extra clothes instead of throwing them out. Finally, *recycle* plastic, glass, metal cans, and paper. These materials can be turned into new items to sell instead of clogging up a landfill. If we all work together and practice "reduce, reuse, recycle," Earth will be a cleaner, better place for years to come.

1. What is the main idea of this story?
    a. Keeping Earth clean is important for everyone.
    b. Fresh vegetables taste better than packaged ones.
    c. Earth has too much trash.

2. Why is it important to take care of Earth?

    _____

    _____

3. How can you reduce the amount of waste you produce?

    _____

4. What are some materials you can reuse?

    _____

5. What are some things that can be recycled?

    _____

6. How will Earth be cleaner if we all reduce, reuse, and recycle?

    _____

    _____

Read the story. Then, answer the questions.

Alicia's Song

Alicia had been practicing for weeks. She sang in the shower, in her bedroom, and on the way to school. Her teacher said that she was ready to sing in a concert, but Alicia was not sure. Mom had taken her to buy a new dress. She helped Alicia curl her hair. Alicia thought she would feel calm when she walked out onto the stage, but her palms were sweaty and her shoes felt too tight. She hoped she would not forget the words. Alicia heard the applause for the performer before her. Her friend Chelsea walked off the stage and whispered, "You're on!" Chelsea patted Alicia's shoulder and said, "Good luck!" Alicia took a deep breath and walked out into the spotlight. Finally, it was time for her solo. She saw Mom and her teacher smiling at her from the front row and knew she would do well.

1. What is Alicia doing?

   _____

2. How long has Alicia been practicing?

   _____

3. What clues tell you how Alicia feels?

   _____

   _____

4. How did Mom help Alicia prepare?

   _____

5. What does Chelsea do to help Alicia?

   _____

6. How does Alicia feel at the end of the story? How do you know?

   _____

   _____

Read the story. Then, answer the questions.

Dad's Day

Dad's birthday was in June, near Father's Day. Sometimes, they were even on the same day. Isabelle and Hector thought it was unfair when their dad only had one special day in June. Their friends' dads had a Father's Day party in June and a birthday party in a different month. Isabelle thought of a way to fix this problem. They would surprise Dad in autumn with Dad's Day. Hector talked to their mom about cooking a special breakfast. She showed him how to cook eggs and bacon. Isabelle made a special card for Dad. They were careful to keep their plans secret. One day in October, Isabelle and Hector woke up early and crept downstairs. They cooked Dad's breakfast and took it upstairs with their card. Dad loved his surprise. He said that he hoped they could have Dad's Day every weekend!

1. Why do Isabelle and Hector want to have a Dad's Day?

   _____

   _____

2. Why are Dad's birthday and Father's Day on the same day only sometimes?

   _____

3. What does Hector do to prepare?

   _____

4. What does Isabelle do to prepare?

   _____

5. Why do Isabelle and Hector keep their plans secret?

   _____

6. Why does Dad want to have Dad's Day every weekend?

   _____

   _____

Name _____

Read the story. Then, answer the questions.

Training Jake

Lucy had a playful dog named Jake. He liked to grab her toys and run away from her. When Jake was a puppy, it was easy to catch him. As Jake grew bigger, Lucy had to shout for him to come back. Neither of them was having much fun. Lucy's mom thought Jake should go to obedience training. A trainer could show Lucy how to make Jake obey her. Lucy found a class that met at the park on Saturday mornings. She walked Jake down to the park, but she felt like Jake was walking her! He was so strong, she could hardly hold him back. At the park, the other dogs were already sitting politely in a circle. The trainer smiled when Jake and Lucy ran up. She said, "Jake has a lot of energy! I can help both of you learn how to control it."

1. Why is Jake's behavior becoming a problem as he gets bigger?

   _____

   _____

2. What clues tell you that training will be good for both Jake and Lucy?

   _____

3. When and where does the class meet?

   _____

4. Why does Lucy feel like Jake is walking her?

   _____

5. How can you tell the other dogs already know some commands?

   _____

6. Will the trainer be able to help Jake? Why or why not?

   _____

Name _____

Read the story. Then, answer the questions.

A Painting for Mom

Mario loved to paint. He was always asking Mom for money to spend on supplies like brushes and special paper. Sometimes, Mom said that Mario had an expensive talent. Mario was walking home one day when he saw a sign about a city art contest. The topic was "What My Mom Means to Me." The winner would receive a cash prize! Mario thought about all of the art supplies he could buy if he won. As soon as he got home, he got out his paints and brushes. He thought about everything Mom did for their family. She cooked healthy food for him and his sister. She drove them to swimming classes in the summer. She worked hard so that they could buy new shoes when they grew out of their old ones. Mario smiled and started to paint. Now, he had a new idea for what to do with the money if he won.

1. What is Mario doing?

   _____

2. Why does Mom say Mario's art talent is expensive?

   _____

3. What will the winner of the art contest receive?

   _____

4. What does Mario want to do with the prize money?

   _____

5. What does Mom do for Mario's family?

   _____

   _____

6. What might be Mario's new idea for the money at the end of the story?

   _____

Read the story. Then, answer the questions.

Taylor's Tomato Garden

One day, Taylor's class took a field trip to a greenhouse. The students were amazed at how many different plants were growing in the building. There were plump tomatoes and lovely pink orchids. The gardener explained that he kept the greenhouse warm and misty so that the plants could grow better. He said that it was easier to grow plants inside the greenhouse, where they were not in danger from bad weather or pests. When Taylor got home from school, she told her mother all about the greenhouse. She asked if they could build one in their backyard. Wouldn't it be great to have fresh tomatoes year-round? Mom said, "A greenhouse sounds like fun, but it can be a lot of work. Why don't you grow some tomatoes in a pot first to see if you have a green thumb?" Taylor decided to try. She would grow so many tomatoes that they would need a greenhouse to hold them all!

1. What kinds of plants did Taylor's class see?

   _____

2. Why are greenhouses good places to grow plants?

   _____

   _____

3. What does Taylor want to do?

   _____

4. What does Mom suggest?

   _____

5. What does it mean to have a green thumb?

   _____

6. What does Taylor decide to do at the end of the story?

   _____

   _____

Read the story. Then, answer the questions.

Family Photos

Valerie's father had accepted a new job across the country, so he would be leaving soon. Valerie and her mother would be staying in their old house until school was out. Valerie would miss her friends when they moved, but she would miss her dad more. Her mother pretended to be cheerful, but Valerie knew she would be lonely too. Sometimes, she caught her mom looking at old photos with a tear in her eye. She decided to make something that would remind both her mom and her dad that they had a strong family. One afternoon, Valerie took the box of family photos up to her room. She cut out two large cardboard hearts. Then, she picked out pictures of herself, her mom, and her dad. She glued the pictures to the hearts. At the top of each heart she wrote "A Family Is Love." Now Dad would have pictures to remember them by, and Mom would not be so sad when she looked at the photos.

1. Why is Valerie's father moving without them?

   _____

   _____

2. Who will Valerie miss the most?

   _____

3. Why does Mom pretend to be cheerful?

   _____

4. What clues do you have that Mom is not really cheerful?

   _____

5. Why does Valerie cut out two cardboard hearts?

   _____

6. Why will Mom be less sad when she looks at photos now?

   _____

Name _____

Read the story. Then, answer the questions.

Soup Kitchen

Rashad's parents liked to help other people. His mom made recordings of books for the blind, and his dad built new houses for people who could not afford them. Rashad's mother said that they should have Thanksgiving dinner at the soup kitchen. Rashad's dad said that was an excellent idea. Rashad did not know what a soup kitchen was. He liked soup, so maybe it was a place to try lots of different kinds. But they usually ate turkey and stuffing at Thanksgiving. He did not think that soup would taste as good. On Thanksgiving Day, Rashad helped his dad carry boxes to the car. They held canned goods, fresh vegetables, and even a turkey! When they got to the soup kitchen, Rashad discovered that there was more than just soup. The soup kitchen was a place where people could come for dinner if they had no food of their own. Rashad's parents were helping serve dinner. Rashad helped too, and he thought it was the best Thanksgiving ever.

1. How do Rashad's parents help others?

    _____

    _____

2. What does Rashad think a soup kitchen is?

    _____

3. What does Rashad's family usually eat at Thanksgiving?

    _____

4. What clues tell you what a *soup kitchen* really is?

    _____

    _____

5. How do Rashad's parents help at the soup kitchen?

    _____

6. How can you tell Rashad likes helping people too?

    _____

Read the story. Then, answer the questions.

Dad's Trumpet

Owen's dad played the trumpet when he was in school. He led the marching band and had a solo in every concert. Owen wanted to play the trumpet too. One day at Grandma's house, he found a dusty case in the closet of his dad's old room. It was Dad's old trumpet! Grandma said that Owen could try it out, so Owen put the instrument to his lips. He blew as hard as he could, but there was no sound. Grandma showed him how to buzz his lips on the mouthpiece, and finally the trumpet made a noise. It sounded nothing like the players Owen had heard in the band. Owen felt sad. He guessed he did not have his dad's talent. He was about to put the trumpet away, when Grandma stopped him. She smiled and said, "You sound just like your dad did when he first started playing. Don't give up yet!"

1. What clues do you have that Owen's dad was a good trumpet player?

   _____

   _____

2. Why does Owen want to play the trumpet?

   _____

3. How can you tell that Dad does not play the trumpet anymore?

   _____

4. Why does Owen have a hard time playing the trumpet?

   _____

5. Why does Grandma tell Owen not to give up yet?

   _____

   _____

6. What do you think Owen will do next?

   _____

   _____

Read the story. Then, answer the questions.

The Long Hike

Jackie and her friends decided to go on a hike Saturday morning. They wanted to reach the top of a nearby hill so that they could see the whole town. Her mom asked if she had remembered to pack water and some nuts for the trail. Jackie was in a hurry, but she stopped to pick up a bottle of water and a packet of nuts for her backpack. She thought they would be back before she got thirsty or hungry, but it took them more time to get to the top of the hill than she had expected. When they stopped to rest, she heard her stomach growl. The view was nice. Jackie and her friends sat down and ate a snack. When they finished, they jogged down the trail. When they got to the bottom of the hill, Jackie saw her dad's car pull up. He rolled down the window and said with a smile, "Ready for lunch?"

1. Why do Jackie and her friends want to hike up the hill?

   _____

2. How can you tell Jackie's parents want her to be careful on the trail?

   _____

3. What does Jackie take with her?

   _____

4. How can you tell Jackie is glad she brought food and water?

   _____

   _____

5. Why does Jackie's dad come to meet her?

   _____

   _____

6. What do you think Jackie will do the next time she goes on a hike?

   _____

Read the story. Then, answer the questions.

Gavin's New Pet

Gavin wanted a pet more than anything else in the world. Dogs made him sneeze, and cats made his eyes water. Mom said that he could have a fish, but Gavin wanted something furry to pet. Gavin's teacher brought a hamster to school one day. She said that Harry would live in their classroom, but someone would need to take him home over spring break. Gavin's hand shot up in the air. He knew that Mom would think that Harry was wonderful and allow him to have a hamster of his own. Harry's week at Gavin's house was full of adventure. First, he squirmed away from Gavin's little sister when she tried to pet him. Then, he got out of his cage and hid in Gavin's pile of socks. Finally, he chewed up Gavin's science notebook. At the end of the week, Gavin was happy for Harry to go back to school. He said, "Maybe I'll get a fish after all!"

1. Why can't Gavin get a cat or a dog?

   _____

2. What kind of pet does Gavin want?

   _____

3. Why does Harry have to go home with a student?

   _____

4. What does Harry do at Gavin's house?

   _____

   _____

5. Why is Gavin happy to take Harry back to school?

   _____

   _____

6. Why does Gavin decide to get a fish after all?

   _____

   _____

Name _____

Read the story. Then, answer the questions.

Predicting

A.   Sandra's mother offered to help her get ready for the new school year. Sandra had grown a full inch taller over the summer. Her shoes were too tight, and her pants were almost above her ankles.

1. What do you think Sandra and her mother will do?

   _____

2. Which clues helped you decide?

   _____

   _____

B.   When Betsy got home from school, she could not find her cat. Betsy called out her cat's name, but her cat did not come. Betsy looked in her closet. She looked under her bed. Just then, Betsy heard her dad drive up. He was home from work. Betsy was glad her dad was home.

1. What do you think Betsy will do?

   _____

2. Which clues helped you decide?

   _____

   _____

C.   Mandy tried out for the school track team. She wore her favorite shoes and came in first in her race. The gym teacher posted the results the day after the tryouts. Mandy raced to the gym to see the list of who had made the team.

1. What do you think will happen next?

   _____

2. Which clues helped you decide?

   _____

Name _____

Read the story. Then, answer the questions.

Predicting

A.　　Miguel needed to write a book report. He finished reading the book and began to plan his paper. The report was worth two test grades, so it was important for him to do well. Miguel's mom said that he had a phone call. It was his friend Tony, who wanted to play video games.

1.　What do you think will happen next?

_____

2.　Which clues helped you decide?

_____

B.　　Timothy laid his head on his desk. His face felt hot, and the desk was nice and cool. Timothy's class was supposed to have an ice cream party that afternoon. Timothy thought the ice cream would feel good to his sore throat. Just then, his teacher said that she thought Timothy should go to the nurse's office.

1.　What do you think will happen next?

_____

2.　Which clues helped you decide?

_____

C.　　Lynn and her brother Trey decided to go hiking. They wore sturdy shoes and light clothing. They put on hats and plenty of sunscreen. They had just reached the top of a tall, rocky hill when they heard a clap of thunder. The sky grew dark. Trey spotted a cave in the side of the hill.

1.　What do you think will happen next?

_____

2.　Which clues helped you decide?

_____

_____

Name _____

Read the story. Then, answer the questions.

Predicting

A. Angel's teacher told the class to close their math books. They were having a pop test! Angel was surprised. She was happy she had studied the chapter the night before. She had not understood the problems in class, so she had asked her mother for extra help. She took out a sheet of paper and wrote her name at the top.

1. What do you think will happen next?

_____

2. Which clues helped you decide?

_____

B. Brian came home from school and prepared himself a sandwich. He put some slices of meat and cheese on it with extra mustard. Brian put his sandwich on a plate and took it to the living room. He thought he would watch his favorite TV show while he ate. His dog came in to see what Brian was doing. Brian set his sandwich on the table and went back into the kitchen for a glass of milk.

1. What do you think will happen next?

_____

2. Which clues helped you decide?

_____

C. Sarah went to her uncle's farm to visit her cousin, Kami. Sarah and Kami were the same age and wore the same size. Sometimes, people thought they were twins! Kami wanted to go fishing, so she told Sarah to put on old jeans. Then, Sarah realized she had forgotten her suitcase.

1. What do you think will happen next?

_____

2. Which clues helped you decide?

_____

Name _____

Read the story. Then, answer the questions.

Predicting

A.   Raul wanted to earn money this summer. He was tired of asking for change to buy comic books and candy. His best friend, Shane, lived next door. Shane and his family were going to be gone all summer. Shane's family could not travel on the plane with their two dogs.

1. What do you think Raul will do?

    _____

2. Which clues helped you decide?

    _____

    _____

B.   Jan's family was moving to a new town with their orange and white cat. Sadly, the cat ran away when they were moving boxes from the truck to the house. Two weeks later, the cat still had not returned. Jan was very sad. She missed her cat. Her new friend Laura, who lived next door, called Jan one morning to say that she had just seen an orange and white cat in her yard.

1. What do you think will happen next?

    _____

2. Which clues helped you decide?

    _____

C.   Kelsey wanted to surprise her mom with a cake. With Grandma's help, she mixed the ingredients and put the batter in a pan. She turned on the oven and put the pan inside. She set a timer and waited for the cake to bake. Kelsey's mom came home early and called, "What is that wonderful smell?"

1. What do you think will happen next?

    _____

2. Which clues helped you decide?

    _____

    _____

                                                        CD-104305 • © Carson-Dellosa

Name _____

Read the story. Then, answer the questions.

Predicting

A.   Jason stood at the top of the ladder to the diving board. His knees felt wobbly, and his hands were sweaty. He walked out onto the board. It was a long way down. Just then, he heard his sister shout, "Come on, Jason! You can do it!" He took a deep breath.

1. What do you think Jason will do?

_____

2. Which clues helped you decide?

_____

_____

B.   Stephen's stepdad was working late every night. He had not gotten home before dark for the past month. Stephen noticed that the yard was covered in dead leaves. He knew his mom did not like it. She had hurt her leg and could not stand up for very long. Stephen wanted to help.

1. What do you think Stephen will do?

_____

2. Which clues helped you decide?

_____

_____

C.   Lindsey took piano lessons. She liked to play for her mom every night after dinner. Sometimes, her friends came over to sing while she played. Lindsey's piano teacher was having a party for all of her students the next week. She wanted all of her students to play for each other, and one would win a prize.

1. What do you think will happen next?

_____

2. Which clues helped you decide?

_____

Read the story. Then, answer the questions.

Predicting

A. Tara found a pair of sunglasses on the bus. They were bright pink with red lightning bolts on the earpieces. Tara felt like a rock star wearing them. After lunch, Tara put on the sunglasses to go out for recess. An older girl ran up to her and said, "Excuse me, but I think that those are mine." Tara's heart sank.

1. What do you think Tara will do?

   _____

2. Which clues helped you to decide?

   _____

B. Ray wanted to play football more than anything else in the world. There was a new team starting in his neighborhood, and he wanted to try out. His family was concerned that if Ray joined the team, he would not have time to do his homework. His family wanted Ray to have fun, but they also wanted him to do well in school. Ray was sure that he would have time to do his homework and play on the team.

1. What do you think will happen next?

   _____

2. Which clues helped you to decide?

   _____

C. Ivy's grandmother was celebrating her 70th birthday soon. Ivy wanted to get her grandmother a special gift, but she had spent her money on new books instead. Ivy loved reading books about Mexico. Her grandmother had come from Mexico, and she used to read to Ivy when she was little. Lately, her grandmother's eyesight had been failing, and she could no longer see the words on the page.

1. What do you think Ivy will do?

   _____

2. Which clues helped you to decide?

   _____

   _____

Name _____

Read the story. Then, answer the questions.

Predicting

A.   Felipe was a new boy in Ethan's class. He did not speak much English, and the teacher could tell that he needed a little extra help. She asked Ethan to help Felipe understand the words in their homework. Ethan went over to Felipe's house after school. He noticed that Felipe's room was covered in posters of soccer players. "Wow!" said Ethan. "I have always wanted to learn to play soccer."

1. What do you think will happen next?

    _____

    _____

2. Which clues helped you decide?

    _____

    _____

B.   Bridget's mother worked in a restaurant. She often had to work late. Bridget thought Mom would enjoy working in an office more, but Mom did not know how to use a computer. Bridget saw a flyer at the library about a computer class for adults. The class met on Saturday mornings, when Bridget was usually at dance class. If Mom signed up for the class, there would be no one to watch Bridget's little brother.

1. What do you think Bridget will do?

    _____

2. Which clues helped you decide?

    _____

    _____

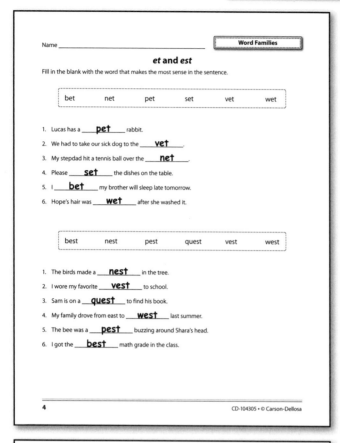

Name _____

et and *est*

Fill in the blank with the word that makes the most sense in the sentence.

bet	net	pet	set	vet	wet

1. Lucas has a __**pet**__ rabbit.
2. We had to take our sick dog to the __**vet**__.
3. My stepdad hit a tennis ball over the __**net**__.
4. Please __**set**__ the dishes on the table.
5. I __**bet**__ my brother will sleep late tomorrow.
6. Hope's hair was __**wet**__ after she washed it.

best	nest	pest	quest	vest	west

1. The birds made a __**nest**__ in the tree.
2. I wore my favorite __**vest**__ to school.
3. Sam is on a __**quest**__ to find his book.
4. My family drove from east to __**west**__ last summer.
5. The bee was a __**pest**__ buzzing around Shara's head.
6. I got the __**best**__ math grade in the class.

4   CD-104305 • © Carson-Dellosa

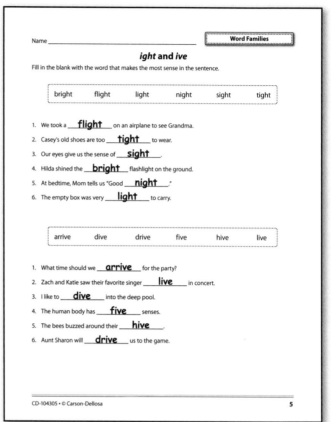

Name _____

ight and *ive*

Fill in the blank with the word that makes the most sense in the sentence.

bright	flight	light	night	sight	tight

1. We took a __**flight**__ on an airplane to see Grandma.
2. Casey's old shoes are too __**tight**__ to wear.
3. Our eyes give us the sense of __**sight**__.
4. Hilda shined the __**bright**__ flashlight on the ground.
5. At bedtime, Mom tells us "Good __**night**__."
6. The empty box was very __**light**__ to carry.

arrive	dive	drive	five	hive	live

1. What time should we __**arrive**__ for the party?
2. Zach and Katie saw their favorite singer __**live**__ in concert.
3. I like to __**dive**__ into the deep pool.
4. The human body has __**five**__ senses.
5. The bees buzzed around their __**hive**__.
6. Aunt Sharon will __**drive**__ us to the game.

CD-104305 • © Carson-Dellosa   5

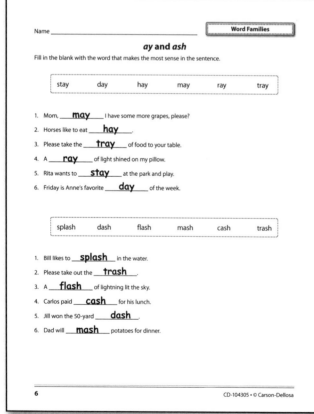

Name _____

ay and *ash*

Fill in the blank with the word that makes the most sense in the sentence.

stay	day	hay	may	ray	tray

1. Mom, __**may**__ I have some more grapes, please?
2. Horses like to eat __**hay**__.
3. Please take the __**tray**__ of food to your table.
4. A __**ray**__ of light shined on my pillow.
5. Rita wants to __**stay**__ at the park and play.
6. Friday is Anne's favorite __**day**__ of the week.

splash	dash	flash	mash	cash	trash

1. Bill likes to __**splash**__ in the water.
2. Please take out the __**trash**__.
3. A __**flash**__ of lightning lit the sky.
4. Carlos paid __**cash**__ for his lunch.
5. Jill won the 50-yard __**dash**__.
6. Dad will __**mash**__ potatoes for dinner.

6   CD-104305 • © Carson-Dellosa

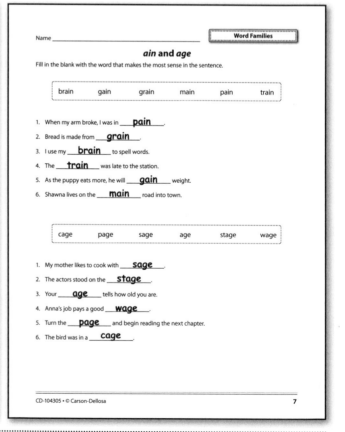

Name _____

ain and *age*

Fill in the blank with the word that makes the most sense in the sentence.

brain	gain	grain	main	pain	train

1. When my arm broke, I was in __**pain**__.
2. Bread is made from __**grain**__.
3. I use my __**brain**__ to spell words.
4. The __**train**__ was late to the station.
5. As the puppy eats more, he will __**gain**__ weight.
6. Shawna lives on the __**main**__ road into town.

cage	page	sage	age	stage	wage

1. My mother likes to cook with __**sage**__.
2. The actors stood on the __**stage**__.
3. Your __**age**__ tells how old you are.
4. Anna's job pays a good __**wage**__.
5. Turn the __**page**__ and begin reading the next chapter.
6. The bird was in a __**cage**__.

CD-104305 • © Carson-Dellosa   7

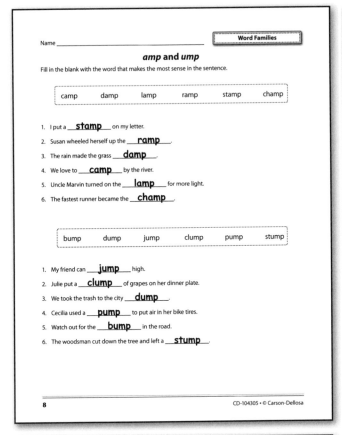

Name _____

Word Families

amp and ump

Fill in the blank with the word that makes the most sense in the sentence.

camp	damp	lamp	ramp	stamp	champ

1. I put a **stamp** on my letter.
2. Susan wheeled herself up the **ramp**.
3. The rain made the grass **damp**.
4. We love to **camp** by the river.
5. Uncle Marvin turned on the **lamp** for more light.
6. The fastest runner became the **champ**.

bump	dump	jump	clump	pump	stump

1. My friend can **jump** high.
2. Julie put a **clump** of grapes on her dinner plate.
3. We took the trash to the city **dump**.
4. Cecilia used a **pump** to put air in her bike tires.
5. Watch out for the **bump** in the road.
6. The woodsman cut down the tree and left a **stump**.

8   CD-104305 • © Carson-Dellosa

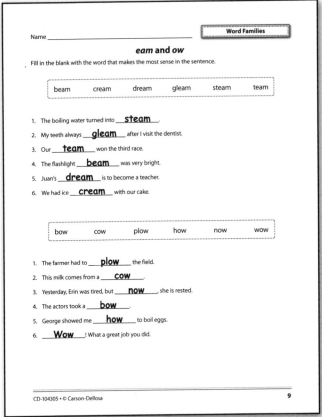

Name _____

Word Families

eam and ow

Fill in the blank with the word that makes the most sense in the sentence.

beam	cream	dream	gleam	steam	team

1. The boiling water turned into **steam**.
2. My teeth always **gleam** after I visit the dentist.
3. Our **team** won the third race.
4. The flashlight **beam** was very bright.
5. Juan's **dream** is to become a teacher.
6. We had ice **cream** with our cake.

bow	cow	plow	how	now	wow

1. The farmer had to **plow** the field.
2. This milk comes from a **cow**.
3. Yesterday, Erin was tired, but **now**, she is rested.
4. The actors took a **bow**.
5. George showed me **how** to boil eggs.
6. **Wow**! What a great job you did.

CD-104305 • © Carson-Dellosa   9

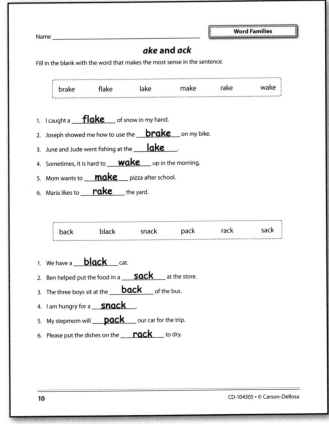

Name _____

Word Families

ake and ack

Fill in the blank with the word that makes the most sense in the sentence.

brake	flake	lake	make	rake	wake

1. I caught a **flake** of snow in my hand.
2. Joseph showed me how to use the **brake** on my bike.
3. June and Jude went fishing at the **lake**.
4. Sometimes, it is hard to **wake** up in the morning.
5. Mom wants to **make** pizza after school.
6. Maria likes to **rake** the yard.

back	black	snack	pack	rack	sack

1. We have a **black** cat.
2. Ben helped put the food in a **sack** at the store.
3. The three boys sit at the **back** of the bus.
4. I am hungry for a **snack**.
5. My stepmom will **pack** our car for the trip.
6. Please put the dishes on the **rack** to dry.

10   CD-104305 • © Carson-Dellosa

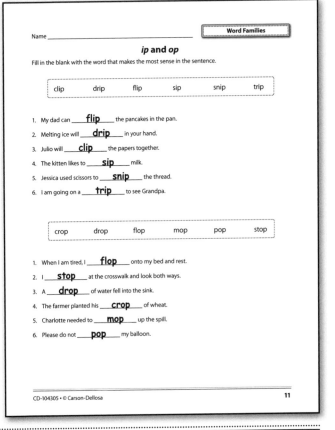

Name _____

Word Families

ip and op

Fill in the blank with the word that makes the most sense in the sentence.

clip	drip	flip	sip	snip	trip

1. My dad can **flip** the pancakes in the pan.
2. Melting ice will **drip** in your hand.
3. Julio will **clip** the papers together.
4. The kitten likes to **sip** milk.
5. Jessica used scissors to **snip** the thread.
6. I am going on a **trip** to see Grandpa.

crop	drop	flop	mop	pop	stop

1. When I am tired, I **flop** onto my bed and rest.
2. I **stop** at the crosswalk and look both ways.
3. A **drop** of water fell into the sink.
4. The farmer planted his **crop** of wheat.
5. Charlotte needed to **mop** up the spill.
6. Please do not **pop** my balloon.

CD-104305 • © Carson-Dellosa   11

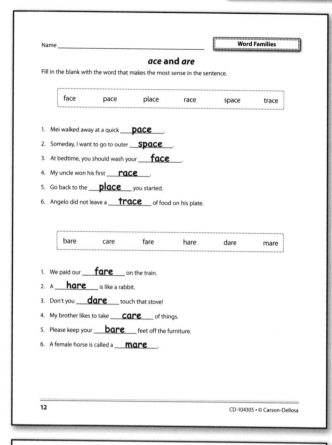

Name _____

Word Families

ace and *are*

Fill in the blank with the word that makes the most sense in the sentence.

face	pace	place	race	space	trace

1. Mei walked away at a quick **pace** .
2. Someday, I want to go to outer **space** .
3. At bedtime, you should wash your **face** .
4. My uncle won his first **race** .
5. Go back to the **place** you started.
6. Angelo did not leave a **trace** of food on his plate.

bare	care	fare	hare	dare	mare

1. We paid our **fare** on the train.
2. A **hare** is like a rabbit.
3. Don't you **dare** touch that stove!
4. My brother likes to take **care** of things.
5. Please keep your **bare** feet off the furniture.
6. A female horse is called a **mare** .

12   CD-104305 • © Carson-Dellosa

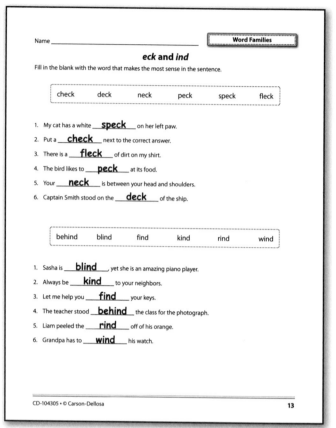

Name _____

Word Families

eck and *ind*

Fill in the blank with the word that makes the most sense in the sentence.

check	deck	neck	peck	speck	fleck

1. My cat has a white **speck** on her left paw.
2. Put a **check** next to the correct answer.
3. There is a **fleck** of dirt on my shirt.
4. The bird likes to **peck** at its food.
5. Your **neck** is between your head and shoulders.
6. Captain Smith stood on the **deck** of the ship.

behind	blind	find	kind	rind	wind

1. Sasha is **blind** , yet she is an amazing piano player.
2. Always be **kind** to your neighbors.
3. Let me help you **find** your keys.
4. The teacher stood **behind** the class for the photograph.
5. Liam peeled the **rind** off of his orange.
6. Grandpa has to **wind** his watch.

CD-104305 • © Carson-Dellosa   13

Name _____

Compound Words

Compound words are two words that have been put together to make a new word. For example, *flash* and *light* can be put together to make the new word *flashlight*. Look at the list of compound words. Fill in each blank in the stories below with the best compound word. Use each word once.

classroom	lunchtime	backpack	seesaw
breakfast	playground	popcorn	homework

My School Day

Mom wakes me up to get dressed and eat **breakfast** . I pack my **backpack** and go to school. I work at my desk in the **classroom** . When it is **lunchtime** , I sit with my friends. At recess, we go to the **playground** . We like to play on the **seesaw** . At the end of the day, our teacher writes our **homework** on the board. After school, I like to eat **popcorn** for a snack.

nighttime	outside	lunchtime	backyard
doghouse	nutshells	butterfly	weekend

Weekend Fun

I like the **weekend** because I get to spend time **outside** with my dog Rusty. In the morning, Rusty comes out of his **doghouse** to play. We play in the **backyard** until **lunchtime** . Rusty likes to bark at the **butterfly** that lives in the garden. He also likes to chew on the **nutshells** that squirrels have dropped from the trees. When **nighttime** comes, Rusty and I are ready to sleep!

14   CD-104305 • © Carson-Dellosa

Name _____

Compound Words

Compound words are two words that have been put together to make a new word. For example, *in* and *side* can be put together to make the new word *inside*. Look at the list of compound words. Fill in each blank in the stories below with the best compound word. Use each word once.

washtub	pancakes	upbeat	goldfish
everything	grandmother	summertime	bedtime

My Grandmother

I like it when my **grandmother** comes to stay with me in the **summertime** . She is an **upbeat** person. She knows how to make **everything** fun. She tells me stories while we make **pancakes** in the morning. We splash each other when she shows me how to wash clothes in a **washtub** . She sings funny songs while we feed my **goldfish** . Grandmother even knows games that make **bedtime** fun!

touchdown	football	kneepads	overtime
newspaper	sometimes	headgear	kickoff

Football

My brother is on the **football** team. He wears special **headgear** and **kneepads** to keep his body safe. I go to watch his games **sometimes** . It is fun to watch the **kickoff** at the beginning of the game. One day, the game went into **overtime** and they had to play longer. My brother scored the winning **touchdown** ! The next day, his picture was in the **newspaper** !

CD-104305 • © Carson-Dellosa   15

Name _____

Compound Words

Compound words are two words that have been put together to make a new word. For example, *when* and *ever* can be put together to make the new word *whenever*. Look at the list of compound words. Fill in each blank in the stories below with the best compound word. Use each word once.

grasshoppers	ladybugs	lunchtime	tablecloth
watermelon	hamburgers	outside	sunglasses

Picnic

My family loves to go __outside__ and have a picnic. Mom spreads out the __tablecloth__ on the ground. At __lunchtime__, Dad serves us __hamburgers__. We eat __watermelon__ for dessert. We watch __grasshoppers__ and __ladybugs__ move through the grass. I put on my __sunglasses__ and play with my sister.

sandbox	storybook	bookshelf	afternoon
oatmeal	bumblebee	bedroom	naptime

Little Sister

My little sister is fun to take care of. She likes to eat __oatmeal__ for breakfast. In the __afternoon__, she likes to play in her __sandbox__. She gets tired and comes in for __naptime__. I take a __storybook__ off the __bookshelf__ and read to her. Her favorite story is about a __bumblebee__. After the story, she goes to sleep in her __bedroom__.

16   CD-104305 • © Carson-Dellosa

Name _____

Compound Words

Compound words are two words that have been put together to make a new word. For example, *thumb* and *print* can be put together to make the new word *thumbprint*. Look at the list of compound words. Fill in each blank in the stories below with the best compound word. Use each word once.

necktie	raincoats	earrings	necklace
briefcase	stepmom	everyone	shoelaces

Getting Ready for the Day

__Everyone__ in my family gets ready for the day in a different way. My __stepmom__ puts on her jewelry, like her __earrings__ and a __necklace__. Dad puts on a __necktie__ and picks up his __briefcase__ to take to work. I just tie my __shoelaces__, and I am ready to go! When the weather is bad, we all do one thing the same. We all put on our __raincoats__!

suitcases	airport	takeoff	gumball
doorway	seatbelt	headphones	airplane

Flying

Last year, Mom and I flew to visit Grandpa. We got to the __airport__ early and put tags on our __suitcases__. When the __airplane__ arrived, we got in line to board. We walked through the __doorway__ of the plane and found our seats. I put on my __seatbelt__, and Mom gave me some __headphones__ so I could listen to music. After __takeoff__, my ears hurt a little, so Mom gave me a __gumball__ to chew.

CD-104305 • © Carson-Dellosa   17

Name _____

Compound Words

Compound words are two words that have been put together to make a new word. For example, *over* and *coat* can be put together to make the new word *overcoat*. Look at the list of compound words. Fill in each blank in the stories below with the best compound word. Use each word once.

butterflies	earthworms	backyard	ladybugs
fireflies	honeybees	everywhere	rainstorm

Insects

Bugs are __everywhere__ you look. __Honeybees__ like to get pollen from flowers. __Butterflies__ have colorful wings. __Ladybugs__ are red with black spots. __Earthworms__ live in the ground and come out after a __rainstorm__. When it is dark, __fireflies__ come out and fly around. It is fun to see them light up in the __backyard__.

underwater	fishhook	catfish	campfire
rowboat	sunshine	something	waterproof

Fishing

My uncle likes to go fishing. He puts on old clothes and __waterproof__ boots and stands by the water. Sometimes, he goes out in a __rowboat__. He puts bait on the __fishhook__ and throws out the line. The hook sinks __underwater__. He waits for the __catfish__ swimming to take the bait. He stands in the __sunshine__ and fishes until he catches __something__. Then, he cooks the fish over a __campfire__.

18   CD-104305 • © Carson-Dellosa

Name _____

Compound Words

Compound words are two words that have been put together to make a new word. For example, *eye* and *lid* can be put together to make the new word *eyelid*. Look at the list of compound words. Fill in each blank in the stories below with the best compound word. Use each word once.

rainstorms	rainwater	weatherman	snowflakes
snowstorms	rainfall	snowmen	thunderclouds

Rain and Snow

The __weatherman__ tells us what weather we can expect. In the spring, we usually have __rainstorms__ with lots of dark __thunderclouds__. Our garden needs the __rainfall__, and we like to collect __rainwater__ to water our plants with later. During winter, we usually get __snowstorms__! We watch the white __snowflakes__ fall. Later, we go outside and play in the snow. We even make __snowmen__!

someday	shoemaker	schoolteacher	firefighter
anything	hairdresser	lawmaker	salesperson

Jobs

What job would you like to have __someday__ when you are an adult? A __shoemaker__ makes and fixes shoes. A __schoolteacher__ works with children. A __hairdresser__ cuts people's hair. Both a police officer and a __firefighter__ help people. A __salesperson__ sells things. A __lawmaker__ works in an office. Girls and boys can be __anything__ they choose!

CD-104305 • © Carson-Dellosa   19

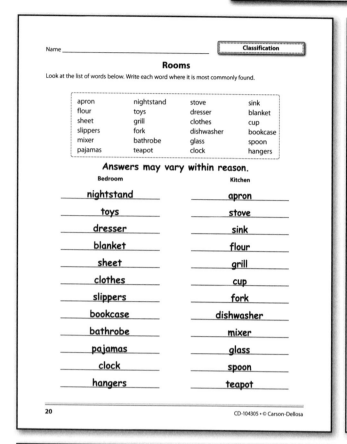

Name _____

Classification

Rooms

Look at the list of words below. Write each word where it is most commonly found.

apron	nightstand	stove	sink
flour	toys	dresser	blanket
sheet	grill	clothes	cup
slippers	fork	dishwasher	bookcase
mixer	bathrobe	glass	spoon
pajamas	teapot	clock	hangers

Answers may vary within reason.

Bedroom	Kitchen
nightstand	apron
toys	stove
dresser	sink
blanket	flour
sheet	grill
clothes	cup
slippers	fork
bookcase	dishwasher
bathrobe	mixer
pajamas	glass
clock	spoon
hangers	teapot

20

CD-104305 • © Carson-Dellosa

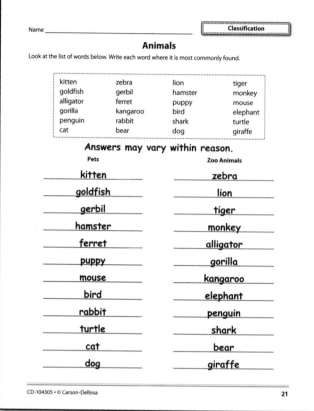

Name _____

Classification

Animals

Look at the list of words below. Write each word where it is most commonly found.

kitten	zebra	lion	tiger
goldfish	gerbil	hamster	monkey
alligator	ferret	puppy	mouse
gorilla	kangaroo	bird	elephant
penguin	rabbit	shark	turtle
cat	bear	dog	giraffe

Answers may vary within reason.

Pets	Zoo Animals
kitten	zebra
goldfish	lion
gerbil	tiger
hamster	monkey
ferret	alligator
puppy	gorilla
mouse	kangaroo
bird	elephant
rabbit	penguin
turtle	shark
cat	bear
dog	giraffe

CD-104305 • © Carson-Dellosa

21

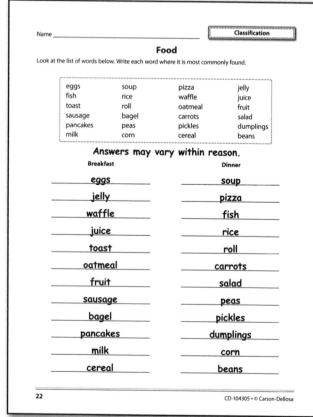

Name _____

Classification

Food

Look at the list of words below. Write each word where it is most commonly found.

eggs	soup	pizza	jelly
fish	rice	waffle	juice
toast	roll	oatmeal	fruit
sausage	bagel	carrots	salad
pancakes	peas	pickles	dumplings
milk	corn	cereal	beans

Answers may vary within reason.

Breakfast	Dinner
eggs	soup
jelly	pizza
waffle	fish
juice	rice
toast	roll
oatmeal	carrots
fruit	salad
sausage	peas
bagel	pickles
pancakes	dumplings
milk	corn
cereal	beans

22

CD-104305 • © Carson-Dellosa

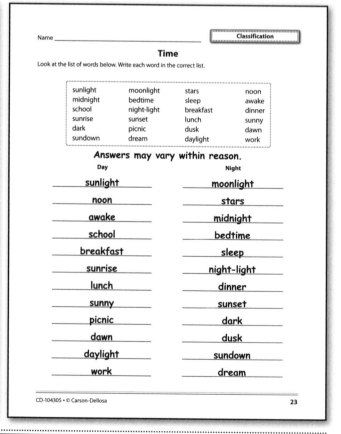

Name _____

Classification

Time

Look at the list of words below. Write each word in the correct list.

sunlight	moonlight	stars	noon
midnight	bedtime	sleep	awake
school	night-light	breakfast	dinner
sunrise	sunset	lunch	sunny
dark	picnic	dusk	dawn
sundown	dream	daylight	work

Answers may vary within reason.

Day	Night
sunlight	moonlight
noon	stars
awake	midnight
school	bedtime
breakfast	sleep
sunrise	night-light
lunch	dinner
sunny	sunset
picnic	dark
dawn	dusk
daylight	sundown
work	dream

CD-104305 • © Carson-Dellosa

23

Name _____

Classification

Weather

Look at the list of words below. Write each word in the correct list.

umbrella	snowman	skiing	thunder	lightning
bright	hot	cold	wet	snowball
dry	sprinkle	drops	flakes	icy
puddle	clouds	sun	sunglasses	winter
summer	splash	mittens	swimming	raincoat
clear	shining	blazing	arctic	shovel

Answers may vary within reason.

Sunny	Snowy	Rainy
bright	snowman	umbrella
hot	skiing	thunder
dry	cold	lightning
sun	snowball	wet
sunglasses	flakes	sprinkle
summer	icy	drops
swimming	winter	puddle
clear	mittens	clouds
shining	arctic	splash
blazing	shovel	raincoat

CD-104305 • © Carson-Dellosa

Name _____

Classification

Senses

Look at the list of words below. Write each word in the correct list.

eyes	nose	ears	scent	hear
see	perfume	flower	cookies	picture
radio	television	movie	concert	barking
crying	odor	song	voice	glasses
skunk	loud	yellow	noise	eyelid
watch	lemon	view	trash	soap

Answers may vary within reason.

Sight	Sound	Smell
eyes	ears	nose
see	hear	scent
picture	radio	perfume
television	concert	flower
movie	barking	cookies
glasses	crying	odor
yellow	song	skunk
eyelid	voice	lemon
watch	loud	trash
view	noise	soap

CD-104305 • © Carson-Dellosa

Name _____

Classification

Sports

Look at the list of words below. Write each word in the correct list.

pool	glove	bases	kick	field
mound	bat	swimsuit	goggles	team
water	ball	pitcher	score	dive
throw	underwater	slide	goal	float
coach	pass	goalie	dugout	

Answers may vary within reason.

Swimming	Soccer	Baseball
pool	kick	glove
swimsuit	field	bases
goggles	team	mound
water	score	bat
dive	ball	dugout
underwater	goalie	pitcher
slide	pass	coach
float	goal	throw

CD-104305 • © Carson-Dellosa

Name _____

Homophones

Homophones

Homophones are words that sound alike but are spelled differently. The words also mean different things. Choose the correct homophone for each sentence.

| bare | bear | heel | heal | tale | tail |

1. Joey hurt the __heel__ of his foot when he stepped on a stone.
2. My favorite __tale__ is the story about Jack and the giant.
3. A __bear__ lives in the woods and likes to eat honey.
4. Doctors try to __heal__ people.
5. Kurt stuck his __bare__ feet in the swimming pool.
6. Her dog wags its __tail__ when it is happy.

| fair | fare | maid | made | weak | week |

1. My family went to the state __fair__.
2. What is your favorite day of the __week__?
3. A __maid__ is someone who helps with cleaning and serving.
4. After Uma won the race, her legs felt __weak__.
5. The bus __fare__ is one dollar.
6. Julia __made__ a picture frame for her stepdad.

CD-104305 • © Carson-Dellosa

Name _____

Homophones

Homophones

Homophones are words that sound alike but are spelled differently. The words also mean different things. Choose the correct homophone for each sentence.

too	two	to	cent	scent	sent

1. The __two__ kittens played with the ball of yarn.
2. A penny equals one __cent__ .
3. My aunt asked me to go __to__ the store.
4. Malcolm __sent__ a letter to his friend.
5. I will clean my desk and the table __too__ .
6. The flower has a sweet __scent__ .

I	eye	you	ewe	wear	where

1. My friend and __I__ ate lunch together.
2. The __ewe__ took care of her lamb.
3. You can see many things with your __eye__ .
4. Do you know __where__ to put the books away?
5. Would __you__ please hand me that pencil?
6. Hillary will __wear__ her blue shoes today.

28
CD-104305 • © Carson-Dellosa

Name _____

Homophones

Homophones

Homophones are words that sound alike but are spelled differently. The words also mean different things. Choose the correct homophone for each sentence.

bury	berry	hare	hair	ate	eight

1. Jen will be __eight__ years old tomorrow.
2. Mom put a fresh __berry__ in each glass of lemonade.
3. Some people __ate__ dinner before they went to the game.
4. In the story, the fox and the __hare__ had a race.
5. Our dog likes to __bury__ the bones we give him.
6. Mark's sister has long brown __hair__ .

main	mane	wrap	rap	four	for

1. The horse's __mane__ was hard to brush.
2. Please __wrap__ the gift in pretty paper.
3. I have __four__ people in my family.
4. Dad went __for__ a walk in the park.
5. We heard a __rap__ at the door.
6. Dave lives on the __main__ road in his town.

CD-104305 • © Carson-Dellosa
29

Name _____

Homophones

Homophones

Homophones are words that sound alike but are spelled differently. The words also mean different things. Choose the correct homophone for each sentence.

one	won	here	hear	hire	higher

1. We are __here__ to learn.
2. My brother hopes they __hire__ him for the job.
3. David had __one__ sticker left, and he gave it to his friend.
4. The plane flew __higher__ than the kite.
5. Do you __hear__ a band playing music?
6. Chan ran fast and __won__ the race.

know	no	meet	meat	pause	paws

1. My cat washes her face using her __paws__ .
2. Maria added __meat__ to the taco.
3. Did you __know__ that ice is frozen water?
4. The students will __meet__ after school to play games.
5. Please __pause__ so I do not miss anything.
6. There are __no__ apples left on the tree.

30
CD-104305 • © Carson-Dellosa

Name _____

Homophones

Homophones

Homophones are words that sound alike but are spelled differently. The words also mean different things. Choose the correct homophone for each sentence.

course	coarse	groan	grown	rose	rows

1. My uncle's beard is very __coarse__ .
2. When I am fully __grown__ , I want to be a nurse.
3. Larry gave his stepmom a __rose__ for her birthday.
4. The pain in my leg made me __groan__ .
5. The farmer planted 10 new __rows__ of corn.
6. Of __course__ you may have more soup!

stare	stair	read	red	pail	pale

1. I sat on the bottom __stair__ in front of the building.
2. I used a __pail__ and sand to make a sand castle.
3. Our teacher __read__ a story to us after lunch.
4. The light brown chair looked __pale__ next to the dark brown chair.
5. My cat likes to __stare__ out the window.
6. Ling wore a bright __red__ dress in the play.

CD-104305 • © Carson-Dellosa
31

Name _____

Homophones

Homophones are words that sound alike but are spelled differently. The words also mean different things. Choose the correct homophone for each sentence.

| right | write | sail | sale | root | route |

1. The **root** of a tooth is below the gum.
2. Mark the **right** answer on your paper.
3. Captain Juan will **sail** the boat to shore.
4. The sign says that the car is for **sale**.
5. Lilly liked taking the faster **route** to school.
6. I will **write** a story about my town.

| our | hour | side | sighed | weather | whether |

1. We will be home in an **hour**.
2. The **weather** is beautiful today!
3. Taylor **sighed** when she sat in her chair.
4. My family loves **our** house.
5. Sheila painted one **side** of the fence purple.
6. Harry wondered **whether** or not he should take an umbrella.

32   CD-104305 • © Carson-Dellosa

Name _____

Homophones

Homophones are words that sound alike but are spelled differently. The words also mean different things. Choose the correct homophone for each sentence.

| due | do | dew | seize | seas | sees |

1. The fisherman sailed the seven **seas**.
2. A fun thing to **do** is to visit the creek.
3. Sherry's library book is **due** on Monday.
4. Josh **sees** his grandparents every weekend.
5. When you **seize** something, you grab it.
6. We smelled the morning **dew** in the air.

| pair | pare | pear | rain | reign | rein |

1. The king will **reign** for his whole life.
2. When you have a **pair** of something, you have two of them.
3. The cool **rain** felt good on our hot faces.
4. To make the horse slow down, pull on the **rein**.
5. Would you like an apple or a **pear**?
6. Mom will **pare** the potatoes before cooking them.

CD-104305 • © Carson-Dellosa   33

Name _____

Using Context Clues

When you come to a word and you do not know the meaning, use context clues to help you figure it out. Context clues are the other words around the word you do not know.

Use context clues to figure out the meaning of each underlined word below. Circle the correct meaning.

1. My brother and I often argue about who gets to use the computer.
   a. work   (b.) disagree   c. study

2. The official told us not to enter the building until 8 o'clock.
   (a.) person in charge   b. nurse   c. child

3. Josie saw an unusual light in the sky and asked her teacher what it was.
   a. dark   b. star   (c.) different

4. The cardinal in my backyard is a beautiful sight. I love its bright color and sweet song.
   a. singer   b. branch   (c.) bird with red feathers

5. Mom asked me to turn down the volume on the radio because it was too loud.
   (a.) noise level   b. book   c. color

6. You will need to separate the reading papers from the math papers.
   a. put together   (b.) set apart   c. teach

7. It is hard to balance in the middle of a seesaw without falling off.
   a. ride   (b.) stay steady   c. walk

8. If you soak a raisin in water overnight, it will swell to the size of a grape.
   (a.) grow   b. drown   c. wonderful

34   CD-104305 • © Carson-Dellosa

Name _____

Using Context Clues

When you come to a word and you do not know the meaning, use context clues to help you figure it out. Context clues are the other words around the word you do not know.

Use context clues to figure out the meaning of each underlined word below. Circle the correct meaning.

1. My style is to wear T-shirts and jeans, but my sister wears fancy dresses.
   a. clothes   (b.) fashion   c. boots

2. I avoid eating snacks before dinnertime.
   (a.) stay away from   b. love   c. try to have

3. Lucy's family permits her to walk home with a friend.
   a. bans   b. drives   (c.) allows

4. The journey from my house to Grandma's takes five hours.
   (a.) trip   b. airplane   c. car

5. My brother built a model airplane. Then, he painted it red and blue.
   a. real   b. person who shows off clothes   (c.) toy

6. Everyone loves her friendliness and charm.
   a. voice   (b.) nice manner   c. necklace

7. Please notify the coach today if you would like to try out for the team.
   (a.) tell   b. obey   c. play for

8. One element of a successful day is getting enough sleep.
   a. start   b. chemical   (c.) part

CD-104305 • © Carson-Dellosa   35

Worksheet (page 36)

Name _____ Context Clues

Using Context Clues

When you come to a word and you do not know the meaning, use context clues to help you figure it out. Context clues are the other words around the word you do not know.

Use context clues to figure out the meaning of each underlined word below. Circle the correct meaning.

1. The car tire scraped the curb as it went around the corner.
   (a.) edge of a road   b. sidewalk   c. boots

2. We went on a march through the neighborhood.
   a. month   b. band   (c.) walk

3. After Jerry ate the entire pizza, his stomach hurt.
   (a.) whole   b. wheel   c. small

4. Polar bears live in arctic weather.
   a. very hot   b. rainy   (c.) very cold

5. My stepmom is helping me study so I can improve my grades.
   a. study   (b.) raise   c. read

6. My teacher invites families to observe her class so that they know how she teaches.
   (a.) watch   b. leave   c. teach

7. The motion of the rocking boat made me feel ill.
   a. ocean   b. captain   (c.) movement

8. The motor is at the rear of the boat, just behind the seats.
   a. side   (b.) back   c. middle

36   CD-104305 • © Carson-Dellosa

Worksheet (page 37)

Name _____ Context Clues

Using Context Clues

When you come to a word and you do not know the meaning, use context clues to help you figure it out. Context clues are the other words around the word you do not know.

Use context clues to figure out the meaning of each underlined word below. Circle the correct meaning.

1. The principal reason for studying is to learn new things.
   (a.) main   b. school   c. last

2. The teacher will accept our homework until tomorrow morning.
   a. stay away from   b. give away   (c.) take

3. We tried all morning, but it was impossible to get tickets to the game.
   a. certain   b. easy   (c.) not possible

4. Mr. Loy told us the good news with a grin on his face.
   a. cheerful   (b.) smile   c. sad

5. Joey put the photograph in a silver frame.
   (a.) picture holder   b. question   c. snapshot

6. What is your individual opinion about the food?
   a. class   (b.) own   c. thought

7. My uncle is a soldier in the military.
   (a.) armed forces   b. officer   c. government

8. Corrie chose the ordinary name Spot for her Dalmatian puppy.
   a. unusual   (b.) normal   c. correct

CD-104305 • © Carson-Dellosa   37

Worksheet (page 38)

Name _____ Context Clues

Using Context Clues

When you come to a word and you do not know the meaning, use context clues to help you figure it out. Context clues are the other words around the word you do not know.

Use context clues to figure out the meaning of each underlined word below. Circle the correct meaning.

1. Marcy wanted to magnify the words on the bottle so that she could see them better.
   (a.) make bigger   b. copy   c. read

2. Each person is wearing a label with his or her name on it.
   a. jacket   b. shirt   (c.) tag

3. It is not nice to tease people or animals.
   a. obey   b. talk to   (c.) bother

4. When water is heated, steam rises into the air.
   (a.) droplets   b. ice   c. lakes

5. Mr. Jones conducts the choir when they give a concert.
   a. behavior   (b.) leads   c. does experiments

6. It is always nice to see a familiar face.
   a. unknown   b. belonging to parents   (c.) something that is known

7. Our school's teachers want to educate all of their students.
   (a.) teach   b. study   c. watch

8. It is always best to be honest in what you do and say.
   a. be funny   (b.) tell the truth   c. lie about

38   CD-104305 • © Carson-Dellosa

Worksheet (page 39)

Name _____ Context Clues

Using Context Clues

When you come to a word and you do not know the meaning, use context clues to help you figure it out. Context clues are the other words around the word you do not know.

Use context clues to figure out the meaning of each underlined word below. Circle the correct meaning.

1. In North America, people vote to elect their leaders of government.
   a. object to   (b.) choose   c. win

2. The majority of the class voted to have pizza instead of sandwiches for lunch.
   (a.) most people   b. few people   c. teachers

3. My mom's greatest concern is that we get home safely.
   a. rule   b. problem   (c.) worry

4. A bride often wears a veil on her head during a wedding.
   (a.) net that goes over the face   b. long gown   c. flowers

5. You should always be civil to other students and teachers.
   a. quiet   b. rude   (c.) polite

6. The new pool is private. Only people who live in that neighborhood can use it.
   a. open   (b.) not public   c. fun

7. The scent of some flowers makes my nose itch.
   a. sound   b. sight   (c.) smell

8. I will wrap a gift for Mario to open at his party.
   a. buy   b. speak about   (c.) put paper around

CD-104305 • © Carson-Dellosa   39

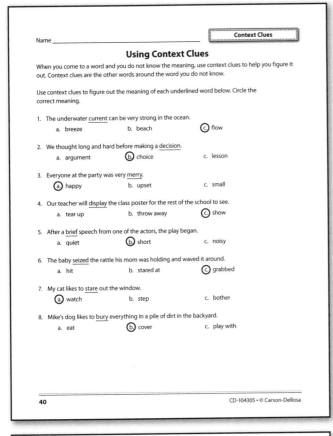

Context Clues

Name _____

Using Context Clues

When you come to a word and you do not know the meaning, use context clues to help you figure it out. Context clues are the other words around the word you do not know.

Use context clues to figure out the meaning of each underlined word below. Circle the correct meaning.

1. The underwater current can be very strong in the ocean.
   a. breeze   b. beach   **c. flow**

2. We thought long and hard before making a decision.
   a. argument   **b. choice**   c. lesson

3. Everyone at the party was very merry.
   a. happy   b. upset   c. small

4. Our teacher will display the class poster for the rest of the school to see.
   a. tear up   b. throw away   **c. show**

5. After a brief speech from one of the actors, the play began.
   a. quiet   **b. short**   c. noisy

6. The baby seized the rattle his mom was holding and waved it around.
   a. hit   b. stared at   **c. grabbed**

7. My cat likes to stare out the window.
   a. watch   b. step   c. bother

8. Mike's dog likes to bury everything in a pile of dirt in the backyard.
   a. eat   **b. cover**   c. play with

40   CD-104305 • © Carson-Dellosa

Context Clues

Name _____

Using Context Clues

When you come to a word and you do not know the meaning, use context clues to help you figure it out. Context clues are the other words around the word you do not know.

Use context clues to figure out the meaning of each underlined word below. Circle the correct meaning.

1. Before it rains, I can feel the moisture in the air.
   a. thunder   b. sunshine   **c. wetness**

2. The bark on a tree is very rough.
   a. outer covering   b. leaves   c. sand

3. I groaned when I realized that I had forgotten my book.
   a. shouted   b. whispered   **c. sighed loudly**

4. My sister beamed when our mother said, "Good job!"
   a. shined a ray of light   **b. smiled broadly**   c. frowned

5. The fare for riding the train was a dollar for adults.
   a. ticket price   b. store   c. railroad

6. The crowd rumbled like thunder as the news spread.
   a. jumped   b. screamed   **c. roared**

7. My hand felt weak after I finished writing the report.
   a. strong   **b. tired**   c. loose

8. The effect of staying up all night was that I fell asleep at breakfast.
   a. result   b. cause   c. change

CD-104305 • © Carson-Dellosa   41

Context Clues

Name _____

Using Context Clues

When you come to a word and you do not know the meaning, use context clues to help you figure it out. Context clues are the other words around the word you do not know.

Use context clues to figure out the meaning of each underlined word below. Circle the correct meaning.

1. Dad likes to make a special tomato sauce to put on our pizza.
   a. bowl   b. dinner   **c. topping**

2. Drop the noodles into the pan when the water starts to boil.
   a. stir   **b. heat**   c. freeze

3. My mom and stepdad had to sign a special form to buy our house.
   a. paper   b. book   c. name

4. After I finished eating, my plate was bare.
   a. large animal   **b. empty**   c. plenty

5. I like wearing skirts because they are pretty when I twirl.
   a. spin   b. don't like   **c. enjoy**

6. The surface of the water was calm until it began to rain.
   a. stormy   **b. still**   c. wavy

7. Jimmy liked the glory of winning the city's big race.
   a. honor   b. flag   c. medal

8. My friend and I are opposites, but we still have fun together.
   a. happy   b. exactly alike   **c. not alike**

42   CD-104305 • © Carson-Dellosa

Context Clues

Name _____

Using Context Clues

When you come to a word and you do not know the meaning, use context clues to help you figure it out. Context clues are the other words around the word you do not know.

Use context clues to figure out the meaning of each underlined word below. Circle the correct meaning.

1. Shelby is on a quest to find her watch.
   a. wheel   b. race   **c. search**

2. Two world wars were fought during the 20th century.
   a. season   **b. period of 100 years**   c. month

3. The first 13 U.S. states formed a union so that they could be stronger.
   a. separation   b. president   **c. single governing body**

4. In the story, the fox chased the hare across the field.
   a. rabbit   b. frog   c. something on your head

5. In our society, everyone must follow certain laws.
   a. house   **b. community**   c. rules

6. Todd ate lunch in the pause between speakers.
   a. break   b. animals' feet   c. nap

7. Anna exclaimed in a loud voice, "I got an A on the test!"
   a. sang   b. read   **c. shouted**

8. James glanced at my friend across the classroom.
   a. words   **b. looked**   c. spoke

CD-104305 • © Carson-Dellosa   43

Name _____

Read the story. Then, answer the questions.

Amelia Earhart

Amelia Earhart is famous for being the first woman to fly an airplane across the Atlantic Ocean. She was born in 1897 and saw her first airplane at the Iowa state fair at age 10. Although she studied to be a nurse and then a social worker, she was always interested in flight. She started taking flying lessons in 1921 and then bought her first plane. Since the aircraft was bright yellow, she called it Canary. In 1928, Earhart flew from Canada to Wales, crossing the Atlantic Ocean in only 21 hours. When she returned to the United States, a parade was held in her honor. She crossed the Atlantic again in 1932, this time by herself. After this accomplishment, the U.S. Congress gave her a special medal called the Distinguished Flying Cross. Earhart continued to set new records, and in 1937 she decided to fly around the world. Her plane was lost over the Pacific Ocean, and Earhart was never heard from again.

1. What is the main idea of this story?
   a. Amelia Earhart flew around the world.
   b. Amelia Earhart was a brave woman who flew airplanes.
   c. Amelia Earhart had a yellow plane called Canary.

2. When was Earhart born?
   1897

3. Where did Earhart see her first airplane?
   at the Iowa state fair

4. Why did Earhart call her first plane Canary?
   It was bright yellow.

5. Why did Earhart receive a medal?
   She was the first woman to fly across the Atlantic.

6. What happened to Earhart in 1937?
   Her plane was lost over the Pacific Ocean while she was trying to fly around the world.

Name _____

Read the story. Then, answer the questions.

Thomas Jefferson

Thomas Jefferson was an important figure in early U.S. history. He was born in 1743 in the colony of Virginia. He became a lawyer and then grew active in the government of the new country that would become the United States. In 1776, he helped write the U.S. Declaration of Independence, which said that the American colonies were no longer tied to Great Britain. He served as governor of Virginia and then went to France to help strengthen ties between the two countries. Jefferson became the third president of the United States and served two terms from 1801 to 1809. During his presidency, Jefferson authorized the Louisiana Purchase, which expanded U.S. territory to include over 800,000 square miles from Canada to the Gulf Coast. Jefferson died in 1826, but people in the United States are reminded of him every time they spend a nickel. Jefferson's face is on one side, and his home, Monticello, is on the other.

1. What is the main idea of this story?
   a. Thomas Jefferson was an important person in U.S. history.
   b. Thomas Jefferson's face is on the nickel.
   c. Thomas Jefferson was a lawyer.

2. Where was Jefferson born?
   Virginia

3. What did Jefferson do in 1776?
   helped write the U.S. Declaration of Independence

4. Why did Jefferson go to France?
   to strengthen ties between France and the United States

5. When did Jefferson serve as president of the United States?
   from 1801 to 1809

6. How did the Louisiana Purchase change the United States?
   It increased the size by 800,000 square miles, from Canada to the Gulf Coast.

Name _____

Read the story. Then, answer the questions.

Sandford Fleming

What time is it? Before the work of Sandford Fleming, it could be hard to tell. Fleming was born in Scotland in 1827. He moved to Canada, where he drew up plans for a railroad from the east coast to the west coast. He worked to promote the use of iron bridges rather than wood because he thought iron bridges were safer. In 1851, he designed the first Canadian postage stamp, which was worth three cents and had a picture of a beaver on it. In 1876, Fleming was traveling in Ireland when he missed his train. The schedule said that the train would leave at 11 o'clock in the evening, but it left at 11 o'clock in the morning instead. To avoid this kind of problem, Fleming suggested that countries around the world use a single 24-hour clock. By 1929, most of the world's countries had adopted time zones that fit into this measurement of time.

1. What is the main idea of this story?
   a. Sandford Fleming was Scottish but lived in Canada.
   b. Sandford Fleming came up with the idea for standardized time.
   c. Sandford Fleming missed a train in Ireland.

2. What did Fleming draw up plans for in Canada?
   a railway from the east coast to the west coast

3. Why did Fleming prefer iron bridges to wooden ones?
   He thought iron bridges were safer.

4. What did the first Canadian stamp look like?
   It had a beaver on it.

5. Why did Fleming miss his train?
   The schedule had an evening time printed instead of a morning one.

6. How did Fleming's ideas change the way people tell time today?
   Today, countries are divided into time zones that fit into a single 24-hour clock.

Name _____

Read the story. Then, answer the questions.

Alexander Graham Bell

Alexander Graham Bell is known as the inventor of the telephone. He was born in 1847 in Edinburgh, Scotland. At the age of 12, after his mother lost her hearing, Bell became interested in studying sound. Bell learned to use sign language so that he could talk to her. He traveled to the United States as an adult and worked as a teacher for people who could not hear. He conducted experiments on how sound travels, which led to his invention of the telephone. In 1876, he was able to speak into one end of his machine. His assistant, Thomas Watson, heard him at the other end, even though he was in another room. The first sentence spoken over the telephone was, "Mr. Watson, come here, I want to see you." The Bell Telephone Company was created shortly afterward, and by 1886 there were over 150,000 phones in use in the United States. Bell died in 1922, but his invention lives on today.

1. What is the main idea of this story?
   a. Thomas Watson was Bell's assistant.
   b. The first telephone call was made in 1876.
   c. Alexander Graham Bell invented the telephone.

2. When was Bell born?
   1847

3. Why was Bell interested in studying sound?
   His mother lost her hearing.

4. What led to Bell's invention of the telephone?
   his experiments on how sound travels

5. What was the first sentence said on a telephone?
   "Mr. Watson, come here, I want to see you."

6. What can you conclude about how Bell's invention helped people talk to each other?
   People no longer had to be in the same room to talk to each other.; They could talk across great distances.

Name _____

Read the story. Then, answer the questions.

Martin Luther King, Jr.

Martin Luther King, Jr., was an important leader in the U.S. civil rights movement. The civil rights movement forced leaders to change laws so that all people would be treated fairly, regardless of their skin color. King was born in 1929 in Atlanta, Georgia. In 1954, King became the leader of a church in Montgomery, Alabama. During this time, African Americans were told that they had to give up their bus seats if a white person wanted to sit down. King and others refused to ride the buses at all until they were given equal treatment. In 1963, he led a march in Washington, D.C., to ask the government to change the laws so that everyone was treated fairly. King received the Nobel Peace Prize in 1964 for his work. He traveled to Memphis, Tennessee, in 1968 to give a speech in support of equal wages. He was shot on April 4. Although King died, his ideas on freedom and equality live on today.

1. What is the main idea of this story?
   a. Martin Luther King, Jr., was a great civil rights leader.
   b. Martin Luther King, Jr., led a march in 1963.
   c. Martin Luther King, Jr., was born in 1929.

2. Where was King born?
   Atlanta, Georgia

3. What did African Americans have to do on the buses in the 1950s?
   They had to give up their seats if a white person wanted to sit down.

4. Why did King lead a march in Washington, D.C.?
   to ask the government to change the laws to be fair

5. What happened on April 4, 1968?
   King was shot in Memphis, Tennessee.

6. What did the civil rights movement do?
   forced leaders to change laws so that all people would be treated fairly

48   CD-104305 • © Carson-Dellosa

Name _____

Read the story. Then, answer the questions.

Elisha Otis

Have you ever ridden on an elevator? Elevators make it much easier for people to get from one floor to another in a tall building. At one time, elevators were not as safe as they are today. Elisha Otis helped change that. Early elevators used ropes that sometimes broke, sending the people riding the elevator to the ground. People could be hurt. Otis made wooden guide rails to go on each side of the elevator. Cables ran through the rails and were connected to a spring that would pull the elevator back up if the cables broke. Otis displayed his invention for the first time at the New York Crystal Palace Exhibition in 1853. His safety elevators were used in buildings as tall as the Eiffel Tower in Paris, France, and the Empire State Building in New York City. Otis died in 1861. His sons, Charles and Norton, continued to sell his design, and many elevators today still have the Otis name on them.

1. What is the main idea of this story?
   a. The Otis family still sells elevators today.
   b. At one time, elevators were unsafe to use.
   c. Elisha Otis found a way to make elevators safe.

2. Why were early elevators dangerous?
   The ropes often broke, sending people to the ground.

3. What did the spring in Otis's elevators do?
   stopped the elevator from crashing if the cables broke

4. When and where was Otis's elevator displayed for the first time?
   1853 at the New York Crystal Palace Exhibition

5. What are two buildings that used Otis's elevator design?
   the Eiffel Tower and the Empire State Building

6. What did Otis's sons do after his death?
   They continued to sell his design.

CD-104305 • © Carson-Dellosa   49

Name _____

Read the story. Then, answer the questions.

Susan B. Anthony

You may know the name Susan B. Anthony from the U.S. dollar coin, but she was famous long before the coin was made. Anthony was a leader who worked for women's rights in the 19th and 20th centuries. She grew up in the Northeast of the United States and was educated at home after a teacher refused to teach her math because she was a girl. Anthony became a teacher and fought for equal wages for women. She attended a special meeting in New York, along with many others, and then began speaking publicly about women's rights. In 1869, Anthony and Elizabeth Cady Stanton formed a group called the National Women's Suffrage Association, which worked to gain women the right to vote. Anthony died in 1906, but American women finally gained the right to vote in 1920, when the Nineteenth Amendment to the U.S. Constitution was passed. Anthony was honored in 1979 with a dollar coin bearing her image.

1. What is the main idea of this story?
   a. Susan B. Anthony could not learn to do math.
   b. Susan B. Anthony worked for women's rights.
   c. A dollar coin honored Susan B. Anthony in 1979.

2. When did Anthony work for women's rights?
   in the 19th and early 20th centuries

3. Why was Anthony educated at home?
   A teacher refused to teach her math.

4. What did Anthony fight for as a teacher?
   equal wages for women

5. What did the National Women's Suffrage Association do?
   worked to gain women the right to vote

6. What happened in 1920?
   The Nineteenth Amendment was passed, giving American women the right to vote.

50   CD-104305 • © Carson-Dellosa

Name _____

Read the story. Then, answer the questions.

Lucy Maud Montgomery

Lucy Maud Montgomery is famous for creating the character of Anne Shirley in her widely read series *Anne of Green Gables*. Montgomery was born in 1874 on Prince Edward Island in Canada. She lived with her grandparents and went to class in a one-room schoolhouse. Her first poem was published when she was only 17 years old. She taught at three island schools and took courses at a university in Nova Scotia. She wrote *Anne of Green Gables* in 1905, but it was not published until 1908. The book became a bestseller, and Montgomery wrote several other books based on the main character. Two films and at least seven TV shows have been made from the *Anne* books. Although Montgomery moved away from Prince Edward Island in 1911, all but one of her books are set there. Many people today still visit the island to see where "Anne Shirley" grew up.

1. What is the main idea of this story?
   a. Lucy Maud Montgomery grew up on Prince Edward Island.
   b. Lucy Maud Montgomery is famous for writing *Anne of Green Gables*.
   c. Lucy Maud Montgomery was a schoolteacher.

2. Who is Anne Shirley?
   a character in Montgomery's *Anne of Green Gables* series

3. What was Montgomery's early life like?
   She lived with her grandparents and went to class in a one-room schoolhouse.

4. When was Montgomery's first poem published?
   when she was 17 years old

5. How can you tell that *Anne of Green Gables* was a popular book?
   Two films and at least seven TV shows have been made from it.

6. Why do many people visit Prince Edward Island today?
   to see where the character Anne Shirley grew up

CD-104305 • © Carson-Dellosa   51

Name _____

Read the story. Then, answer the questions.

Roberto Clemente

Roberto Clemente was born in Puerto Rico in 1934. He played baseball in his neighborhood as a child and played for his high school team. He joined a junior national league when he was only 16. He played baseball briefly in Canada before signing to play for the Pittsburgh Pirates in 1954. Clemente served in the U.S. Marine Reserves for several years, which helped him grow physically stronger. He helped the Pirates win two World Series. During the off-season, Clemente often went back to Puerto Rico to help people there. He liked visiting children in hospitals to give them hope that they could get well. After the country of Nicaragua was hit by an earthquake in 1972, Clemente directed relief efforts there. At age 38, he was on his way to deliver supplies to Nicaragua when his plane crashed. He was elected to the Baseball Hall of Fame in 1973. He was the first Hispanic player to receive the honor.

1. What is the main idea of this story?
   a. Roberto Clemente was a great baseball player who also helped people.
   b. Roberto Clemente died in a plane crash.
   c. Roberto Clemente was elected to the Baseball Hall of Fame.

2. Where was Clemente born?
   Puerto Rico

3. Where did Clemente play baseball?
   Puerto Rico, Canada, Pittsburgh

4. What did Clemente do during the off-season?
   visited Puerto Rico to help people, visited children in hospitals to give them hope

5. What happened in Nicaragua in 1972?
   An earthquake hit the country.

6. Why was Clemente flying to Nicaragua?
   He was on his way to deliver supplies.

52   CD-104305 • © Carson-Dellosa

Name _____

Read the story. Then, answer the questions.

Lady Bird Johnson

Lady Bird Johnson was born as Claudia Taylor in 1912. She received her nickname after a nurse said that she was as pretty as a ladybird beetle, another name for a ladybug. Lady Bird married Lyndon Baines Johnson in 1934, and together they had two daughters. After President John F. Kennedy's death in 1963, Lyndon Johnson became president of the United States and Lady Bird became First Lady. Most women who serve as First Lady choose a special project to work on. Lady Bird chose to make the highways of the United States more beautiful. She helped get millions of flowers planted, which we can still see today. Lady Bird believed that "where flowers bloom, so does hope." She continued to help make her home state of Texas more beautiful after her husband left office. The Lady Bird Johnson Wildflower Center in Austin, Texas, was opened to help visitors learn about native plants.

1. What is the main idea of this story?
   a. Lady Bird Johnson was born in 1912.
   b. Lady Bird Johnson was married to a president.
   c. Lady Bird Johnson helped make America's highways beautiful.

2. What was Lady Bird Johnson's given name?
   Claudia Taylor

3. How did Lady Bird get her nickname?
   A nurse said she was as pretty as a ladybird beetle, or ladybug.

4. How did Lady Bird become the First Lady?
   Her husband became president after President John F. Kennedy died.

5. What does the Wildflower Center in Austin, Texas, do?
   helps visitors learn about native plants

6. What did Lady Bird accomplish as First Lady?
   She helped make the U.S. highways beautiful.

CD-104305 • © Carson-Dellosa   53

Name _____

Read the story. Then, answer the questions.

James Naismith

Have you ever played basketball with your friends? You dribble the ball, run down the court, and shoot it through a hoop. The modern game of basketball was invented by James Naismith, a Canadian gym teacher, in 1891. Naismith wanted a game that would not take up too much room and that could be played indoors. He nailed peach baskets at both ends of the gym and sorted his players into two teams of nine each. The players passed a ball to each other and threw it into the basket when they reached the end of the court. Eventually, players started to bounce the ball instead of just tossing it to each other. This bouncing motion became known as dribbling. Basketball soon caught on among both men's and women's teams. It became an official Olympic sport in 1936, and Naismith was invited to watch. Naismith died in 1939, but his sport lives on. Over 300 million people around the world play basketball today.

1. What is the main idea of this story?
   a. James Naismith's sport lives on today.
   b. James Naismith was a gym teacher.
   c. James Naismith invented the sport of basketball.

2. What are three things players do in basketball?
   Sample answer: dribble the ball, run down the court, and shoot it through a hoop

3. What kind of game did Naismith want to invent?
   an indoor game that took little space to play

4. What did the first basketball hoops look like?
   peach baskets nailed to both ends of the gym

5. In the early days of the sport, what did basketball players do before they learned to dribble?
   tossed the ball to each other

6. How can you tell that basketball is still popular today?
   Over 300 million people play basketball today.

54   CD-104305 • © Carson-Dellosa

Name _____

Read the story. Then, answer the questions.

Babe Didrikson Zaharias

Babe Didrikson Zaharias was an outstanding sportswoman. She played golf, basketball, and baseball and also ran track. Zaharias grew up playing sports with her six brothers and sisters in Port Arthur, Texas. She played basketball with a company team when she worked as a secretary. She joined the U.S. Olympic team and won medals in three track-and-field events at the 1932 Olympics in Los Angeles. Zaharias began playing golf in 1935, and in 1938 she became the first woman to play in a PGA (Professional Golf Association) game. She became famous for her playing, and in 1950 she helped form the LPGA (Ladies Professional Golf Association). This group continues to hold golf matches for female golfers today. Zaharias died in 1956, but she was named to the U.S. Olympic Hall of Fame in 1983. People can learn more about Zaharias's life by visiting a museum in her honor in Beaumont, Texas.

1. What is the main idea of this story?
   a. Babe Didrikson Zaharias grew up in Texas.
   b. Babe Didrikson Zaharias was good at many sports.
   c. Babe Didrikson Zaharias died in 1956.

2. Which sports did Zaharias play?
   golf, basketball, baseball, track and field

3. What happened to Zaharias at the 1932 Olympics?
   She won three medals in track and field.

4. What did Zaharias do in 1938?
   became the first woman to play in a PGA game

5. What honor did Zaharias receive in 1983?
   She was named to the U.S. Olympic Hall of Fame.

6. What does the LPGA do today?
   holds golf matches for female golfers

CD-104305 • © Carson-Dellosa   55

Answer Key

Name _____
Reading about History

Read the story. Then, answer the questions.

Edward R. Murrow

Edward R. Murrow was an American journalist who became famous during the Second World War. He was born in 1908 in North Carolina. After college, Murrow began working for a radio station. People all over America listened to his live broadcasts from the bombing of London, England, in September 1939, known as the Blitz. Before Murrow's reports, people in the United States could only learn about the war through newsreels in movie theaters or articles in newspapers. Now, they could listen to Murrow on their radios at home. Murrow was very brave to risk his life so that Americans could learn about the war in London. After the war ended, Murrow continued to work as a reporter in radio and then in television. On TV, he became known for interviewing, or asking questions of, famous people. Other newscasters followed in Murrow's footsteps, and today we still look forward to hearing from reporters in other countries and listening in on their chats with famous people.

1. What is the main idea of this story?
   a. Edward R. Murrow was a brave American journalist.
   b. Edward R. Murrow talked to many famous people.
   c. Edward R. Murrow worked in London.

2. What type of company did Murrow work for?
   a radio station

3. What was special about Murrow's broadcasts in 1939?
   He broadcast live from London while it was being bombed.

4. How did people learn about the war before Murrow's work?
   through newsreels in movie theaters or articles in newspapers

5. What did Murrow do after the war ended?
   continued to work as a reporter in radio and then television

6. How did Murrow change the way journalists work?
   They started reporting live from different countries and started interviewing famous people.

56   CD-104305 • © Carson-Dellosa

Thomas Edison

Without Thomas Alva Edison, we might all be sitting around in the dark! Although people before Edison worked on designs for the lightbulb, he is credited with creating the modern electric light. Edison was born in 1847. He worked as a telegraph operator. Edison liked working on the night shift so that he could have plenty of time to read and conduct experiments during the day. He invented the phonograph, or record player, in 1877. Edison built his own lab at Menlo Park, New Jersey, where he could continue to work on his inventions. The lab covered the space of two city blocks. Edison showed his lightbulb to the public in 1879. At this time, most people used candles to light their homes. The candles sometimes caused house fires. By 1887, over 100 power plants were sending electricity to customers. Edison registered over 1,000 patents, or designs, for different inventions. It is no wonder that a newspaper called him the Wizard of Menlo Park!

1. What is the main idea of this story?
   a. Thomas Edison built his own lab.
   b. Thomas Edison was a successful American inventor.
   c. Thomas Edison worked on the night shift.

2. What are two of Edison's inventions?
   phonograph, lightbulb

3. Why did Edison like working on the night shift?
   He had plenty of time to read and conduct experiments during the day.

4. How large was Edison's lab at Menlo Park?
   It covered two city blocks.

5. How many different inventions did Edison create?
   over 1,000

6. How did the lightbulb change people's lives?
   They no longer had to use candles to light their homes. Electric lights are safer.

CD-104305 • © Carson-Dellosa   57

Harriet Tubman

Harriet Tubman was a brave woman. Tubman grew up as a slave in Maryland but escaped north to Philadelphia, Pennsylvania, as an adult. She returned to Maryland to help rescue her family and returned again and again to help other slaves. She guided them to safe houses along a network known as the Underground Railroad. People who helped slaves move to safety were called "conductors," after the people who controlled trains on railroads. In 1861, the United States began fighting the Civil War, which was partly a struggle between northern and southern states over whether people should be allowed to own slaves. In 1863, President Abraham Lincoln signed a law stating that slavery was no longer allowed in the United States. With the law on her side, Tubman continued to help people who were treated unfairly until her death in 1913.

1. What is the main idea of this story?
   a. Harriet Tubman was a former slave.
   b. Harriet Tubman lived in Maryland.
   c. Harriet Tubman helped people on the Underground Railroad.

2. What did people in Tubman's time believe about slavery?
   Many people believed that slavery was wrong, but some Americans still owned slaves.

3. Why did Tubman return to Maryland?
   to help rescue her family and help other slaves escape

4. What was the Underground Railroad?
   a network of safe houses for slaves trying to escape

5. What did conductors on the Underground Railroad do?
   helped move slaves to safety

6. What was the Civil War?
   partly a struggle between northern and southern states over whether people should be allowed to own slaves

58   CD-104305 • © Carson-Dellosa

Titanic

In the spring of 1912, a luxury ship called the *Titanic* set off from England on its first journey. The *Titanic* was headed for New York City, but on the night of April 14, its journey was cut short. Around midnight, the ship hit an iceberg, and in less than three hours the ship had sunk. Although over 700 people survived the disaster, more than 1,500 lives were lost in the icy waters of the Atlantic. Because of the way the *Titanic* was built, everyone thought it was impossible for the ship to sink. This certainty led to several of the causes of the disaster. We now know that the captain had ignored warnings of ice and pushed the *Titanic* too fast through dangerous waters. We also know that there were not enough lifeboats for everyone on board. Because of the *Titanic* disaster, new rules were set. Now people know that every ship can sink and so there must be a space in a lifeboat for every person on a ship.

1. What is the main idea of this story?
   a. The *Titanic* was unsinkable.
   b. The sinking of the *Titanic* was a huge disaster.
   c. A ship called the *Titanic* left England in 1912.

2. How was the *Titanic's* journey cut short?
   The ship hit an iceberg and sank.

3. Why did everyone think that it was impossible for the *Titanic* to sink?
   because of the way it was built

4. What does the story say led to several causes of the disaster?
   the certainty that it wouldn't sink

5. What could the captain have done to help avoid this disaster?
   paid attention to warnings

6. What might have been different if the *Titanic* had had enough lifeboats for everyone?
   More people, and maybe everyone on board, could have been saved.

CD-104305 • © Carson-Dellosa   59

Name _____

Read the story. Then, answer the questions.

Elijah McCoy

You may have heard something referred to as "the real McCoy." This expression means "the real thing" instead of a copy. Some people think that "the real McCoy" was Elijah McCoy, who was born in Canada in 1843. His parents were former slaves who escaped from Kentucky to Canada. At the time, slavery was illegal in Canada but not in the United States. McCoy traveled to Scotland when he was 16 to learn how to design, build, and repair machines. After the Civil War ended, he moved to Michigan, where he worked on the railroad. He had to pour oil into the engine whenever the train stopped. McCoy worked on inventions at his home machine shop, where he came up with the idea for a better way to carry oil into train engines. His invention helped trains run more smoothly. Railroad workers would ask for "the real McCoy" because it was better than other machines like it.

1. What is the main idea of this story?
   a. Elijah McCoy created a tool to keep train engines running.
   b. Elijah McCoy was "the real McCoy" that the saying refers to.
   c. Elijah McCoy spent several years in Scotland.

2. What does the phrase "the real McCoy" mean?
   the real thing instead of a copy

3. Why did McCoy's parents move to Canada?
   They were former slaves who escaped from Kentucky.
   Slavery was illegal in Canada but not the United States.

4. Why did McCoy travel to Scotland?
   to learn how to design, build, and repair machines

5. What did McCoy's invention do?
   carried oil into engines so that trains ran more smoothly

6. Why did workers ask for "the real McCoy"?
   It was better than other machines like it.

CD-104305 • © Carson-Dellosa

Name _____

Read the story. Then, answer the questions.

Louisa May Alcott

For nearly 150 years, children have grown up reading about Meg, Jo, Beth, and Amy, in Louisa May Alcott's famous book *Little Women*. Alcott grew up with three sisters in Massachusetts. Like the girls in the book, Alcott and her sisters liked to put on plays for their friends. Her family was very poor, and Alcott helped them by working as a maid, a teacher, a nurse, and finally a writer. Her books about the March family, beginning with *Little Women*, were widely read during her lifetime. The main character, Jo, based on Alcott herself, works as a writer until she marries and has a family. Alcott continued to write until her death in 1888. She also spoke out for women's rights and against slavery. Today, people can visit Orchard House, the home where Alcott grew up and where *Little Women* is set.

1. What is the main idea of this story?
   a. Louisa May Alcott was very poor as a child.
   b. Louisa May Alcott had three sisters.
   c. Louisa May Alcott based her books on her own life.

2. How was Alcott's family like the March family?
   They both had four girls. They both liked to put on
   plays for their friends.

3. How did Alcott help her family?
   by working as a maid, a teacher, a nurse, and a
   writer

4. Who was the character of Jo based on?
   Louisa May Alcott

5. What was Alcott known for besides writing?
   speaking out for women's rights and against slavery

6. How was Alcott different from the character Jo in *Little Women*?
   Jo gave up writing when she got married, but Alcott
   wrote for her whole life.

CD-104305 • © Carson-Dellosa

Name _____

Read the story. Then, answer the questions.

Wayne Gretzky

Wayne Gretzky is called "The Great One" by fans of Canadian hockey. He scored over 1,000 goals during his career. Gretzky was born in Brantford, Ontario, and learned to ice-skate on his family's farm when he was three. Gretzky's father taught him and his three brothers to play hockey on a frozen pond in the backyard. When Gretzky was six, he joined a league of 10-year-olds and began playing on a team. In the summer, he played baseball and lacrosse. He started playing for a professional hockey team, the Indianapolis Racers, when he was 17. He played for the Edmonton Oilers in Canada for nine years, during which they won hockey's Stanley Cup four times. He also played for several U.S. teams. Gretzky retired from the sport in 1999 and was voted into the Hockey Hall of Fame. Both his hometown of Brantford and his adopted city of Edmonton named streets after Gretzky to honor him.

1. What is the main idea of this story?
   a. Wayne Gretzky was a great hockey player.
   b. Wayne Gretzky had three brothers.
   c. Wayne Gretzky played hockey in the United States and Canada.

2. Why is Gretzky called "The Great One" by Canadian hockey fans?
   He scored over 1,000 goals during his career.

3. Where did Gretzky first play hockey?
   on a frozen pond in his backyard with his brothers

4. What other sports did Gretzky play?
   baseball and lacrosse

5. How did Gretzky help the Edmonton Oilers?
   He helped them to win the Stanley Cup four times.

6. What are three honors that Gretzky received?
   He was voted into the Hockey Hall of Fame and had
   two streets named after him.

CD-104305 • © Carson-Dellosa

Name _____

Read the story. Then, answer the questions.

Computers

Have you ever used a computer at school, at the library, or at home? Today's computers can fit on a desktop or in your lap. Computers of the past took up a whole room! One of the first computers was called the ENIAC, which stood for Electronic Numerical Integrator and Calculator. It took up 1,800 square feet (about 167 square meters), weighed nearly 50 tons, and cost $500,000. The ENIAC took three years to build and was designed for the U.S. Army. It required a team of six people to program it, or tell it what to do. The ENIAC was used from 1947 to 1955. In contrast, a personal computer today can weigh as little as two pounds (about one kilogram) and can be operated by one person at a time. The builders of the ENIAC may never have believed students could do their homework on a computer.

1. What is the main idea of this story?
   a. The ENIAC was an early computer.
   b. Computers of the past were very different from ones today.
   c. Students can do their homework on computers.

2. What does *ENIAC* stand for?
   Electronic Numerical Integrator and Calculator

3. How large was ENIAC?
   took up 1,800 square feet and weighed nearly 50 tons

4. What does the word *program* mean in this story?
   a. build a computer
   b. require six people to use
   c. tell a computer what to do

5. When was the ENIAC used?
   from 1947 to 1955

6. How are computers today different from those of the past?
   Computers today are much smaller, lighter, and easier
   to use.

CD-104305 • © Carson-Dellosa

Name _____

Read the story. Then, answer the questions.

Food Webs

A food web is a drawing that shows how different living things are connected. On the web drawing, it shows which animals at the top eat the animals directly below them, and so on until the bottom of the web. For example, a food web might start at the bottom with plants like grass and nuts, which do not eat other living things. Above these plants might be small animals such as mice and insects. Larger animals like owls and snakes eat the smaller animals. A food web can tell you what might happen if different plants or animals disappear from an ecosystem, or the surroundings in which all of these things live. In the food web described above, if something happened to the grass, then the mice and insects would not have much food. This would affect the owls and snakes, which would also not have enough food. Soon, there would be fewer of every animal. This is why it is important to protect all living things in an ecosystem, not just the largest ones.

1. What is the main idea of this story?
   (a.) Food webs show how all living things are connected.
   b. Owls and snakes are the most important animals.
   c. Only the animals at the top should be protected.

2. What is a food web?

   a drawing that shows how living things are connected

3. What is at the bottom of a food web?

   plants like grass or nuts that do not eat other living things

4. What might happen if the insects in a food web were gone?

   The animals that eat insects would soon be gone too.

5. What is an *ecosystem*?
   a. a food web for very large animals
   (b.) the surroundings where a group of plants and animals live
   c. a place that grows only grass and nuts

6. Why is it important to protect all living things in an ecosystem?

   because all living things are connected within an

   ecosystem

64   CD-104305 • © Carson-Dellosa

Name _____

Read the story. Then, answer the questions.

Science Experiments

Scientists learn about the world by conducting experiments. They take careful notes on the supplies they use and the results they find. They share their findings with others, which leads to everyone learning a little more. You can do experiments too! The library has many books with safe experiments for students. You might work with balloons, water, or baking soda. You might learn about how light travels or why marbles roll down a ramp. Ask an adult to help you set up your experiment and to watch to make sure you are safe. Be sure to wash your hands afterward and clean up the area. Take good notes on your work. You may be able to change just one thing the next time to get a completely different result. Most of all, do not worry if your results are different than you expected. Some of the greatest scientific discoveries were made by mistake!

1. What is the main idea of this story?
   (a.) Children can do experiments too, as long as they are safe.
   b. Scientists often make mistakes that lead to great discoveries.
   c. You should always take good notes when conducting an experiment.

2. What do scientists take notes on?

   the supplies they use and the results they find

3. What happens when scientists share their findings with others?

   Everyone learns a little more.

4. Where can you find information about safe experiments?

   the library and the Internet

5. Why should you ask an adult to help?

   to make sure you are being safe

6. Should you worry if you get different results? Why or why not?

   No; some of the greatest scientific discoveries were

   made by mistake.

CD-104305 • © Carson-Dellosa   65

Name _____

Read the story. Then, answer the questions.

Magnets

A magnet is any object with a magnetic field. This means that it pulls things made of iron, steel, or nickel toward it. If you set a paper clip next to a magnet on a table, the paper clip will move toward the magnet. Every magnet has what is called a north pole and a south pole. The north pole of one magnet will stick to the south pole of another magnet. If you try to push the south poles of two magnets together, they will spring apart. Earth has magnetic poles too. Earth is a big magnet! Earth's magnetic poles are not actual places. They are areas of Earth's magnetic field with a certain property. Although Earth's magnetic poles are different than the poles like the one where polar bears live, its magnetic poles are near these poles. The north pole of a magnet will always try to point toward Earth's north magnetic pole. A piece of camping equipment called a compass works by having a magnetized needle that points to Earth's magnetic north pole. So, if you get lost, you could set the compass on a flat surface and wait for the needle to point north.

1. What is the main idea of this story?
   a. If you get lost in the woods, start walking north.
   b. Compasses work by pointing to the north.
   (c.) Magnets are objects that have magnetic fields.

2. What happens if you put a paper clip next to a magnet?

   The paper clip moves toward the magnet.

3. How is Earth like a magnet?

   They both have a north and a south pole.

4. What happens if you push a north pole and a south pole together?

   They will stick together.

5. What happens if you push two south poles together?

   They will spring apart.

6. How does a compass work?

   It has a magnetized needle that points to Earth's

   magnetic north pole.

66   CD-104305 • © Carson-Dellosa

Name _____

Read the story. Then, answer the questions.

Solid, Liquid, Gas

All matter on Earth exists in one of three states: solid, liquid, or gas. Solids, such as boxes or books, have a certain shape that is hard to change. Liquids, such as lemonade or orange juice, take the shape of the bottle or cup they are in. Gases, such as the air you breathe, spread out to fill the space they are in. It is easy to change water from one state to another. The water that you drink is a liquid. When water is heated, such as in a pot on the stove, it becomes a gas. This gas is known as steam, or vapor. Steam is used in an iron to make clothes smooth. It also can be used in a large machine to make electricity. When water is frozen, such as in a tray in the freezer, it turns into ice. Ice is used to cool down drinks or to help a hurt part of the body heal.

1. What is the main idea of this story?
   a. Steam is heated water.
   (b.) All matter exists as a solid, liquid, or gas.
   c. Ice cubes make water taste better.

2. What are two examples of solids?

   Answers may vary.

3. What are two examples of liquids?

   Answers may vary.

4. What are two examples of gases?

   Answers may vary.

5. What do you call water in the three states of matter?

   drinking water, ice, steam or vapor

6. How are solids, liquids, and gases different from one another?

   Solids have a certain shape, liquids take the shape

   of their bottle or cup, and gases spread out to fill

   their space.

CD-104305 • © Carson-Dellosa   67

Name _____   **Reading about Science**

Read the story. Then, answer the questions.

Tornadoes

A tornado is a funnel cloud that forms over land. It is created when warm air meets cold air, making a thunderstorm. Tornadoes can be very dangerous to both people and things. They can leave a trail of damage one mile (1.6 km) wide and 50 miles (80 km) long. The wind speed can reach over 300 miles (480 km) per hour. People often have little warning of a tornado, but certain parts of the United States have tornadoes more frequently than other parts. The area called "Tornado Alley" covers parts of Texas, Oklahoma, Kansas, Nebraska, Iowa, and South Dakota. Tornadoes are more likely to form in the spring and summer. If the weather reporter says that a tornado has been spotted in your area, stay inside. Go to the lowest level of your home, keep as many walls as possible between you and the outside, and keep the windows closed. Do not leave until you hear that the tornado has passed.

1. What is the main idea of this story?
   a. Tornadoes are formed during thunderstorms.
   b. Tornado Alley is an area where many storms occur.
   c. Tornadoes are dangerous to people and buildings.

2. What is a tornado?
   <u>a funnel cloud that forms when warm air meets cold air in a</u>
   <u>thunderstorm</u>

3. How far can the damage from a tornado reach?
   <u>one mile wide and 50 miles long</u>

4. What are three states that are found in Tornado Alley?
   <u>Answers may vary and can include Texas, Oklahoma, Kansas,</u>
   <u>Nebraska, Iowa, and South Dakota.</u>

5. When are tornadoes more likely to form?
   <u>in the spring and summer</u>

6. What should you do if a tornado is spotted in your area?
   <u>Stay inside. Go to the lowest level of your home. Keep windows</u>
   <u>closed. Do not leave until you hear the tornado has passed.</u>

68   CD-104305 • © Carson-Dellosa

Name _____   **Reading about Science**

Read the story. Then, answer the questions.

Floods

Rain is good for people and plants, but when it rains too much, people may be in danger. A flash flood occurs when a lot of rain falls very quickly, filling up the streets faster than the water can drain away. It is very dangerous to drive in a flash flood, because your car may be swept away. If you live in an area where flooding is likely, listen to the radio or television when it starts to rain. Be ready to leave your home if the newscaster tells you to move to a higher location. Before you leave, turn off all electrical equipment. Move important items to a higher floor, if possible. If you leave on foot, do not walk through moving water. Do not drive through standing water unless it is less than six inches (15.24 cm) deep. After a flood, listen to news reports to find out when you can return home and when the water from your tap will be safe to drink.

1. What is the main idea of this story?
   a. Flash floods can be dangerous and happen suddenly.
   b. Never drive through a flooded area.
   c. Take important items with you when you leave your home.

2. What happens during a flash flood?
   <u>A lot of rain falls quickly, filling the streets with water.</u>

3. What could happen to a car in a flash flood?
   <u>It could be swept away.</u>

4. When should you leave your home?
   <u>if the newscaster tells you to move to a higher location</u>

5. What should you do before leaving your home?
   <u>Turn off all electronics and move important items to a</u>
   <u>higher floor.</u>

6. What should you do after a flood?
   <u>Listen to news reports to find out when you can go</u>
   <u>home and when the water will be safe to drink.</u>

CD-104305 • © Carson-Dellosa   69

Name _____   **Reading about Science**

Read the story. Then, answer the questions.

Glaciers

A glacier is a large, thick mass of ice. It forms when snow hardens into ice over a long period of time. It might not look like it, but glaciers can move. They usually move very slowly, but if a lot of the ice melts at once, the glacier may surge forward, or move suddenly over a long distance. Most glaciers are found in Antarctica, the continent at the South Pole, or in Greenland, which is near the North Pole. Areas with glaciers receive a lot of snowfall in the winter and have cool summers. Most glaciers are located in the mountains, where few people live, but occasionally they can cause flooding in cities and towns. Falling ice from glaciers may block the path of people hiking on a trail farther down on the mountain. Icebergs, or large floating pieces of ice, may break off from glaciers and cause problems for ships at sea.

1. What is the main idea of this story?
   a. Icebergs can be dangerous to ships.
   b. Glaciers are large masses of ice found mainly in the mountains.
   c. People usually live far from glaciers.

2. How does a glacier form?
   <u>when snow hardens into ice over a long period of time</u>

3. What does the word *surge* mean in this story?
   a. move forward suddenly
   b. freeze into ice
   c. break off from an iceberg

4. Where are most glaciers found?
   <u>in the mountains of Antarctica and Greenland</u>

5. What is the weather like where glaciers are found?
   <u>The winters have a lot of snowfall, and the summers are cool.</u>

6. How can glaciers be dangerous?
   <u>They can cause flooding. Falling ice may block the path of</u>
   <u>hikers on the mountain. Icebergs may break off and cause a</u>
   <u>problem for ships at sea.</u>

70   CD-104305 • © Carson-Dellosa

Name _____   **Reading about Science**

Read the story. Then, answer the questions.

Health and Fitness

Health and fitness are very important for young people. If you start good habits now, you have a better chance of being a healthy adult later. You may go to gym class several times a week, but you should also try to stay fit outside of school. You and your family can make healthy choices together. You can choose fresh fruit for dessert instead of cake. Offer to help make dinner one night and surprise your family by preparing a delicious salad. You can go for a walk together after dinner instead of watching television. Exercising can help wake up your brain so that you can do a good job on your homework. Making healthy choices may seem hard now, but after a while it will feel good.

1. What is the main idea of this story?
   a. Going to gym class is fun.
   b. Making healthy choices is too hard.
   c. Health and fitness are important for you and your family.

2. What might happen if you start good habits now?
   <u>You have a better chance of being a healthy adult.</u>

3. Where should you try to stay fit?
   <u>outside of school</u>

4. What is a better choice than cake for dessert?
   <u>fresh fruit</u>

5. What can you do instead of watching TV after dinner?
   <u>go for a walk with your family</u>

6. How does exercise affect your brain?
   <u>It wakes up your brain so that you can do a good job</u>
   <u>on your homework.</u>

CD-104305 • © Carson-Dellosa   71

Name _____

Read the story. Then, answer the questions.

Reptiles and Amphibians

You may think that lizards and frogs are in the same family, but they are actually quite different. Lizards, snakes, turtles, and crocodiles are all reptiles. Frogs, toads, and salamanders are amphibians. Both amphibians and reptiles are cold-blooded, which means the warmth of their bodies depends on their surroundings. Most animals in both categories lay eggs instead of giving birth to their young. Reptiles lay hard-shelled eggs in nests, but amphibians lay soft-shelled eggs underwater. When reptiles hatch, they look like tiny adults. Amphibian babies like tadpoles, or baby frogs, have to live underwater until they are older. Adult amphibians spend part of their time in the water and part on land. Reptiles feel dry and scaly to the touch. Amphibians feel moist and sticky. Because amphibians can live both in water and on land, they are more at risk for becoming sick from pollution. It is important to keep ponds and lakes clean so that the animals that live there will be safe.

1. What is the main idea of this story?
   a. There are important differences between reptiles and amphibians.
   b. Reptiles are the same as amphibians.
   c. Frogs and lizards belong to different families.

2. What are three animals that are reptiles?
   Answers may vary.

3. What are three animals that are amphibians?
   Answers may vary.

4. How are amphibians and reptiles similar?
   They are cold-blooded and lay eggs.

5. Why is it important to keep ponds and lakes clean?
   so water is clean and keeps animals that live there safe

6. What are three differences between reptiles and amphibians?
   Answers may vary.

72   CD-104305 • © Carson-Dellosa

Name _____

Read the story. Then, answer the questions.

Dolphins and Sharks

Both dolphins and sharks have fins and live in the ocean, but there are many differences between them. Dolphins are mammals, and sharks are fish. Dolphins have smooth, rubbery skin. Like other mammals, they have hair. Dolphins are born with a few whiskers on their chins, though the whiskers may fall out after birth. Shark skin is covered in tough scales that feel like sandpaper and look like tiny teeth. Baby dolphins stay with their mothers for about three years to learn how to hunt. Baby sharks can start hunting by themselves soon after birth. Dolphins have lungs, so they must come to the surface of the water to breathe. A dolphin shoots air through a blowhole on top of its head like a whale. Sharks breathe through gills, so they can stay underwater much longer. People and dolphins may not look much alike, but they have more in common than dolphins and sharks!

1. What is the main idea of this story?
   a. People and dolphins have nothing in common.
   b. Dolphins and sharks look alike but are very different.
   c. Whales and dolphins both have blowholes.

2. How is dolphin skin different from shark skin?
   Dolphin skin is smooth and rubbery, but shark skin has tough scales.

3. Why do baby dolphins stay with their mothers after birth?
   to learn how to hunt

4. Why must dolphins come to the surface of the water?
   to breathe through their blowholes

5. Why can sharks stay underwater for a long time?
   because they have gills instead of lungs

6. What has more in common with dolphins than sharks do?
   Humans have more in common with dolphins than sharks do.

CD-104305 • © Carson-Dellosa   73

Name _____

Read the story. Then, answer the questions.

Turtles and Tortoises

Turtles and tortoises look very similar, and they are both reptiles. They both have shells that they can pull their heads and legs into in case of danger. They both lay eggs, have scales, and are cold-blooded. However, there are some differences between them. Turtles live in or near the water and can hold their breath for a long period of time while they swim. Tortoises live on land, often in areas that are hot and dry. Turtles have flippers or webbed feet that help them swim. Tortoises have hard, scaly feet that are good for walking on rocks and hard ground. They may have claws to help them dig burrows for resting. Turtles eat insects and fish as well as plants, but tortoises eat mostly plants, such as cactus. If you find an animal that looks like a turtle in your backyard, it is most likely a tortoise.

1. What is the main idea of this story?
   a. Reptiles have scales and lay eggs.
   b. Tortoises like to eat lettuce.
   c. Turtles and tortoises are both reptiles but have some differences.

2. What do turtles and tortoises do in case of danger?
   pull their heads and legs into their shells

3. Where do turtles and tortoises live?
   Turtles live in or near the water, but tortoises live on land.

4. How does a turtle's body help it live in the water?
   It can hold its breath for a long time, and its feet help it swim.

5. How do a tortoise's feet help it live on land?
   Its hard, scaly feet are good for walking on rocks, and its claws help it dig burrows.

6. Why would a turtle in your backyard really be a tortoise?
   Tortoises live on land, so if you find a turtle on land, it is most likely a tortoise.

74   CD-104305 • © Carson-Dellosa

Name _____

Read the story. Then, answer the questions.

Sea Urchins

Sea urchins look like pincushions that live under the sea. They have long, thin spines that stick out all over their bodies. Most sea urchins have spines that are about 0.39 to 1.18 inches (1 to 3 cm) long. Sea urchins are found in oceans all over the world. They can be many colors, from green to brown to red. Their bodies are about 4 inches (10 cm) across. They eat dead fish, seaweed, and very tiny plants called algae. Their spines help them trap food. They also use their five tiny teeth to pull plants off rocks. Hundreds of tiny tubes used as feet help them move along the seafloor. Many creatures, including sea otters, crabs, and eels, like to eat sea urchins.

1. What is the main idea of this story?
   a. Sea urchins are interesting animals that live in the ocean.
   b. Sea urchins taste salty and creamy.
   c. Sea urchins look like pincushions.

2. What do sea urchins' spines look like?
   They are long and thin and about 4 inches across.

3. What do sea urchins eat?
   dead fish, seaweed, and tiny plants called algae

4. How do sea urchins get food?
   They trap food with their spines and pull plants off rocks with their five tiny teeth.

5. How do sea urchins move?
   with hundreds of tiny tubes used as feet

6. Which creatures like to eat sea urchins?
   sea otters, crabs, eels

CD-104305 • © Carson-Dellosa   75

Name _____ Reading about Science

Read the story. Then, answer the questions.

Silkworms

Silk is a soft, smooth type of cloth that is used for clothing, bedding, and wall hangings. It comes from silkworm cocoons, which are spun into thread that is then made into cloth. It takes about 3,000 cocoons to make one pound (about 0.5 kg) of silk. Silkworms become moths as adults. Like most insects, silkworms go through four stages. The moth lays its eggs on a mulberry leaf. After a silkworm hatches into a caterpillar, it munches on leaves until it grows to the length of a human finger. After about a month of eating and growing, the worm spins a cocoon of silk around itself. Spinning the cocoon takes about three days. Inside the cocoon, the silkworm changes shape and becomes a pupa. After about three weeks, the pupa turns into a moth. The moth comes out of the cocoon and starts the cycle all over again.

1. What is the main idea of this story?
   a. Silkworm cocoons are spun into thread.
   b. Silkworms turn into moths as adults.
   (c.) Silkworms go through four stages and help make silk.

2. What is silk used for?
   __clothing, bedding, and wall hangings__

3. What are the stages of a silkworm's life?
   __egg, caterpillar, pupa, moth__

4. What do silkworms eat?
   __mulberry leaves__

5. How long does it take to spin a cocoon?
   a. 3,000 days
   (b.) about three days
   c. about three weeks

6. What happens to the silkworm inside the cocoon?
   __It turns into a pupa and then into a moth.__

76   CD-104305 • © Carson-Dellosa

Name _____ Reading about Social Studies

Read the story. Then, answer the questions.

The Olympic Games

In the Olympic Games, people from all over the world gather together to compete in different sports. The original Olympics were held in Greece around 776 BCE. Young men came together every four years to run races of different lengths. Those who won were given wreaths of olive branches. The modern Olympics were first held in 1896 in Greece. In 1996, people decided that the summer and winter Olympic Games should be held in different years. This means that every two years, thousands of people representing over 200 countries come together to compete in either summer or winter sports. Today's winners receive gold, silver, or bronze medals and compete in hundreds of different events. The Olympics give the host countries a chance to show their culture both to the people who come there and to people who watch on TV. The sports may be different than the original Olympics, but the spirit of goodwill and good sportsmanship is still the same.

1. What is the main idea of this story?
   a. The Olympics are held every four years.
   (b.) People come to the Olympics to compete in different sports.
   c. Good sportsmanship is very important at the Olympics.

2. When and where were the first Olympics held?
   __in Greece around 776 BCE__

3. What did winners receive at the early Olympics?
   __wreaths of olive branches__

4. How did the Olympics change in 1996?
   __People decided the summer and winter Olympics should__
   __be held in different years.__

5. What do Olympic winners receive today?
   __gold, silver, or bronze medals__

6. How do the Olympics help people learn about different cultures?
   __Answers may vary.__

CD-104305 • © Carson-Dellosa   77

Name _____ Reading about Social Studies

Read the story. Then, answer the questions.

Flags of the World

A flag tells something special about an area or a group. For example, the U.S. flag has 13 red and white stripes for the first 13 states, and 50 stars on a blue field for the current 50 states. The Canadian flag has a red maple leaf on white between two bands of red. The maple leaf stands for the nature found in Canada. Canadian provinces and U.S. states also have their own flags. The state flag of Texas has a large white star on blue on the left and two bands of red and white on the right. Because of the flag's single star, Texas is called the Lone Star State. The flag of the Canadian province of New Brunswick has a gold lion on a red field above a sailing ship. The lion stands for ties to Brunswick, Germany, and the British king. The ship represents the shipping industry. The flag of the United Nations, a group of countries that works for world peace, shows a globe surrounded by olive leaves.

1. What is the main idea of this story?
   (a.) Flags tell something special about a country or group.
   b. Some flags have maple leaves or lions on them.
   c. Many flags are red, white, or blue.

2. What does the U.S. flag look like?
   __13 red and white stripes, 50 white stars on a blue__
   __background__

3. What does the Canadian flag look like?
   __red maple leaf on white between two bands of red__

4. Why is Texas called the Lone Star State?
   __Its flag has only one star.__

5. What does the word *field* mean in this story?
   a. an area of grass
   (b.) a large area of a single color
   c. an area of study

6. What does the flag of the United Nations have on it?
   __It has a globe surrounded by olive leaves.__

78   CD-104305 • © Carson-Dellosa

Name _____ Reading about Social Studies

Read the story. Then, answer the questions.

The Continents

Earth is divided into seven large areas of land called continents. The seven continents are Asia, Africa, Australia, Europe, Antarctica, North America, and South America. Each continent is separated from the others by a feature such as an ocean or a mountain range. Continents may be divided into many different countries, states, or provinces. People live on six of the seven continents. The continent of Antarctica is at the South Pole, where the weather is too cold for people to live. Some scientists study in Antarctica at special stations, but many stay there for only part of the year. The largest continent is Asia, which covers over 17,000,000 square miles (44,000,000 square km). The smallest is Australia, which covers nearly 3,000,000 square miles (7,700,000 square km). Asia also has the most people, with a population of over three billion. That accounts for about half the world's people!

1. What is the main idea of this story?
   a. More people live in Asia than on any other continent.
   b. It is hard for people to live in Antarctica.
   (c.) Continents are large areas of land on Earth.

2. List the seven continents.
   __Asia, Africa, Australia, Europe, Antarctica, North__
   __America, South America__

3. What separates continents from each other?
   __features such as oceans or mountain ranges__

4. What is a *station* in the story?
   (a.) a place where scientists study
   b. an area of the classroom
   c. a television channel

5. About how much bigger is Asia than Australia?
   __about 14,000,000 square miles__

6. Why do you think that so many people live in Asia?
   __Answers may vary.__

CD-104305 • © Carson-Dellosa   79

Name _____

Read the story. Then, answer the questions.

Community Helpers

A community is a group of people who live in the same area or have the same interests. Communities need helpers to make them work. Some important community helpers are police officers and firefighters. Police officers make sure everyone is following the rules of the community to keep people safe. Firefighters put out fires and educate people about fire safety. Other community helpers are people who work for the city, such as garbage collectors and park rangers. Garbage collectors drive down city streets to pick up trash that people have put in bags or cans at the curb. Park rangers make sure city parks are clean and safe so that people can play or have picnics in them. Another important helper in the community is a librarian. The librarian makes sure there are lots of good books available for everyone in the community to read. The next time you see a community helper, say "Thank you!"

1. What is the main idea of this story?
   a. A community needs a lot of people to make it work.
   b. Police officers and firefighters are community helpers.
   c. People like to have picnics in city parks.

2. What do police officers do in a community?

   make sure everyone is following the rules to keep
   people safe

3. What do firefighters do in a community?

   put out fires and educate people about fire safety

4. How do garbage collectors help the community?

   They pick up trash that people put out at the curb.

5. Why does a community need park rangers?

   so that the parks are clean and safe to play or have picnics

6. Why should you say "Thank you!" to a community helper?

   Answers may vary.

80   CD-104305 • © Carson-Dellosa

Name _____

Read the story. Then, answer the questions.

World Holidays

You and your family may celebrate several special days a year. People in different countries recognize different holidays. Many people in China have a Lantern Festival to celebrate the new year. They light special lamps and hold colorful parades through the streets. In Scotland, some people celebrate Burns Night, in honor of the Scottish poet Robert Burns. Families or clubs gather together for a special meal and a reading of Burns's poetry on his birthday. While people in the United States celebrate their independence on Independence Day, people in Canada celebrate Canada Day. On July 1, 1867, the government of Canada was created. On both Canada Day and Independence Day, people have community parades and picnics. People in some parts of Germany celebrate Oktoberfest to mark the harvest. They eat traditional German foods like sausage and potato salad. People who went to other countries carried their traditions to their new homes, so many places outside of those countries celebrate the same holidays.

1. What is the main idea of this story?
   a. Burns Night is a special holiday in Scotland.
   b. People around the world celebrate different holidays.
   c. Oktoberfest takes place in many cities.

2. What is a *lantern* in the story?
   a. a type of food eaten in China
   b. a special holiday
   c. a type of lamp

3. How do people in Scotland honor Robert Burns?

   eat a special meal on his birthday and read his poetry

4. How are Independence Day and Canada Day celebrations alike?

   People have community parades and picnics.

5. What does Oktoberfest represent?

   the harvest

6. Why might someone take their traditions to a new country?

   Answers may vary.

CD-104305 • © Carson-Dellosa   81

Name _____

Read the story. Then, answer the questions.

The Right to Vote

Some people think that the most important right of a citizen of a country is the right to vote. Only adults over age 18 are allowed to vote in Canada and the United States. Until the 1970s, only people over 21 could vote! People today can vote for a number of government offices, including the president, vice president, and mayor. They may also vote on laws that affect their city, such as rules about how to use areas of land or what kinds of businesses can be on a given street. In many countries, elections use a secret ballot. This means that no one except the person voting can see who they are voting for. Without a secret ballot, someone might tell you to vote for a certain leader. Each person is allowed to vote only once. This means that everyone gets an equal say in which leaders get elected to office.

1. What is the main idea of this story?
   a. Voting helps people elect their government.
   b. Only adults over 18 can vote.
   c. Everyone has an equal say in government.

2. How did the voting laws change in the 1970s?

   The voting age changed from 21 to 18.

3. Which government offices can people vote for?

   Answers may vary.

4. What kinds of laws can people vote on?

   Answers may vary.

5. What is a *secret ballot*?
   a. a kind of dancing
   b. a vote that no one else can see
   c. a type of song

6. Why is each person only allowed to vote once?

   so that everyone gets an equal say in which leaders
   get elected to office

82   CD-104305 • © Carson-Dellosa

Name _____

Read the story. Then, answer the questions.

City Government

The president and prime minister are important national leaders, but there are also important leaders in your city. Many cities have a mayor, who is responsible for attending events like the opening of a new library or a parade. The mayor often works with a group of people known as a city council. These people come from areas all over the city. They work together to come up with solutions that will work for all citizens. A city may also have a manager, who makes sure that city services are running smoothly day to day. The city manager also creates a budget to show how the city should spend its money. Other members of the city government include the chief of police and the fire chief. These people lead the police and fire departments. They make the rules that all of their employees must follow. A city needs many workers to make a better life for all of its citizens.

1. What is the main idea of this story?
   a. The president is an important leader.
   b. The leader of the police is called a chief.
   c. City government includes many different workers.

2. What does a mayor do?

   Answers may vary.

3. Where do members of a city council come from?

   areas all over the city

4. What does a city manager do?

   makes sure city services are running smoothly, creates
   a budget

5. What is a *budget*?
   a. a report that tells how the city should spend its money
   b. a city manager
   c. a person who leads the fire department

6. Why does a city need many workers?

   to make a better life for all of its citizens

CD-104305 • © Carson-Dellosa   83

346664

33444

322121Answer Key

Answer Key

Planning a City

What do the streets in your city look like? Some cities have streets that are very straight and organized. It is easy to get from one point in the city to another. Other cities have streets that seem to go nowhere. It may be difficult to give directions to your home. When a group of people move to a place and start setting up the streets, they may use something called a grid system. One example of this is found in the city of Philadelphia, Pennsylvania, which is divided into four sections around a central square. The map was laid out by William Penn in 1682. The grid included wide streets that were easy for people to walk down. Penn left London, England, after a fire destroyed most of the city. London had a maze of narrow streets that were hard to move around safely. Penn wanted to make sure people could get around the city easily and safely. Many other cities followed Penn's ideas when setting up their street systems.

1. What is the main idea of this story?
   a. William Penn drew the first grid system.
   b. Planning a city is important for safety.
   c. Some streets are straight and organized.

2. What is one good thing about having straight streets?
   Answers may vary.

3. What is a grid system?
   a. a way of arranging straight streets in a city
   b. a maze of narrow streets
   c. a famous fire in London

4. What is one good thing about having wide streets?
   Answers may vary.

5. Why did Penn leave London?
   because a fire destroyed most of the city

6. How are Philadelphia's streets different from London's?
   Philadelphia has wide streets set up on a grid system, while London's streets are narrow and hard to move around.

84

Musical Cultures

People from different cultures celebrate different holidays and eat different kinds of food. They also have different musical cultures. The United States has many musical traditions. People in New Orleans, Louisiana, in the southern part of the United States, are known for a style of music called jazz. This music has strong rhythms and allows people to play freely. People from a region of the eastern United States called Appalachia play folk music with fiddles and banjos. Much of this music is based on the songs and dance tunes of the British Isles. Countries that border each other have music styles from the people who cross from one country to the other. Some styles from Mexico are *banda* and *cumbia*. Some Canadian styles of music are based on French songs and use accordions and guitars. Because of the radio and television, people all over the world can hear music of other cultures and create new musical traditions of their own.

1. What is the main idea of this story?
   a. Different cultures have different holidays and food.
   b. Some Canadian music is based on French songs.
   c. People have different musical cultures.

2. What is jazz?
   a style of music from New Orleans that has strong rhythms and lets people play freely

3. What is one type of music that has fiddles and banjos?
   folk music from Appalachia

4. What are some styles of music from Mexico?
   banda and cumbia

5. What is some Canadian music based on?
   French songs

6. How do radio and television affect musical cultures?
   They let people hear music from all over the world and create new music of their own.

85

Cleaning Up Earth

There are many cities to live in, but we have only one Earth. It is important to take care of our planet because we cannot move to a new one. You may have heard the phrase "Reduce, reuse, recycle." Putting these words into action will help keep Earth clean. First, try to *reduce* the amount of waste you produce. You can cook with fresh fruits and vegetables instead of packaged foods. Second, *reuse* things when you can. You can make a bird feeder from a milk carton that would otherwise go in the trash. You can also donate your extra clothes instead of throwing them out. Finally, *recycle* plastic, glass, metal cans, and paper. These materials can be turned into new items to sell instead of clogging up a landfill. If we all work together and practice "reduce, reuse, recycle," Earth will be a cleaner, better place for years to come.

1. What is the main idea of this story?
   a. Keeping Earth clean is important for everyone.
   b. Fresh vegetables taste better than packaged ones.
   c. Earth has too much trash.

2. Why is it important to take care of Earth?
   because we cannot move to a new planet; Answers may vary.

3. How can you reduce the amount of waste you produce?
   Answers may vary.

4. What are some materials you can reuse?
   Answers may vary.

5. What are some things that can be recycled?
   plastic, glass, metal cans, paper

6. How will Earth be cleaner if we all reduce, reuse, and recycle?
   Answers may vary.

86

Alicia's Song

Alicia had been practicing for weeks. She sang in the shower, in her bedroom, and on the way to school. Her teacher said that she was ready to sing in a concert, but Alicia was not sure. Mom had taken her to buy a new dress. She helped Alicia curl her hair. Alicia thought she would feel calm when she walked out onto the stage, but her palms were sweaty and her shoes felt too tight. She hoped she would not forget the words. Alicia heard the applause for the performer before her. Her friend Chelsea walked off the stage and whispered, "You're on!" Chelsea patted Alicia's shoulder and said, "Good luck!" Alicia took a deep breath and walked out into the spotlight. Finally, it was time for her solo. She saw Mom and her teacher smiling at her from the front row and knew she would do well.

1. What is Alicia doing?
   performing a song in public

2. How long has Alicia been practicing?
   for weeks

3. What clues tell you how Alicia feels?
   She is nervous. Her palms are sweaty, and her shoes feel tight. She hopes she will not forget the words.

4. How did Mom help Alicia prepare?
   bought her a new dress, curled her hair

5. What does Chelsea do to help Alicia?
   pats her shoulder, tells her "Good luck"

6. How does Alicia feel at the end of the story? How do you know?
   calm; She sees Mom and her teacher smiling at her from the front row and knows she will do well.

87

124

CD-104305 • © Carson-Dellosa

Name _____

Read the story. Then, answer the questions.

Dad's Day

Dad's birthday was in June, near Father's Day. Sometimes, they were even on the same day. Isabelle and Hector thought it was unfair when their dad only had one special day in June. Their friends' dads had a Father's Day party in June and a birthday party in a different month. Isabelle thought of a way to fix this problem. They would surprise Dad in autumn with Dad's Day. Hector talked to their mom about cooking a special breakfast. She showed him how to cook eggs and bacon. Isabelle made a special card for Dad. They were careful to keep their plans secret. One day in October, Isabelle and Hector woke up early and crept downstairs. They cooked Dad's breakfast and took it upstairs with their card. Dad loved his surprise. He said that he hoped they could have Dad's Day every weekend!

1. Why do Isabelle and Hector want to have a Dad's Day?

   Their dad's birthday is close to Father's Day, so he only ever has one special day in June.

2. Why are Dad's birthday and Father's Day on the same day only sometimes?

   Father's Day is not on the same day every year.

3. What does Hector do to prepare?

   learns how to cook eggs and bacon

4. What does Isabelle do to prepare?

   makes a special card for Dad

5. Why do Isabelle and Hector keep their plans secret?

   They want Dad to be surprised.

6. Why does Dad want to have Dad's Day every weekend?

   He would like to have breakfast in bed every weekend.

CD-104305 • © Carson-Dellosa

Name _____

Read the story. Then, answer the questions.

Training Jake

Lucy had a playful dog named Jake. He liked to grab her toys and run away from her. When Jake was a puppy, it was easy to catch him. As Jake grew bigger, Lucy had to shout for him to come back. Neither of them was having much fun. Lucy's mom thought Jake should go to obedience training. A trainer could show Lucy how to make Jake obey her. Lucy found a class that met at the park on Saturday mornings. She walked Jake down to the park, but she felt like Jake was walking her! He was so strong, she could hardly hold him back. At the park, the other dogs were already sitting politely in a circle. The trainer smiled when Jake and Lucy ran up. She said, "Jake has a lot of energy! I can help both of you learn how to control it."

1. Why is Jake's behavior becoming a problem as he gets bigger?

   Lucy cannot catch him when he runs away with her toys.

2. What clues tell you that training will be good for both Jake and Lucy?

   Neither of them has fun when Lucy shouts at Jake.

3. When and where does the class meet?

   Saturday mornings at the park

4. Why does Lucy feel like Jake is walking her?

   He is so strong, she can hardly hold him back.

5. How can you tell the other dogs already know some commands?

   They are already sitting politely in a circle.

6. Will the trainer be able to help Jake? Why or why not?

   Yes; she has a good attitude and smiles at Lucy.

CD-104305 • © Carson-Dellosa

Name _____

Read the story. Then, answer the questions.

A Painting for Mom

Mario loved to paint. He was always asking Mom for money to spend on supplies like brushes and special paper. Sometimes, Mom said that Mario had an expensive talent. Mario was walking home one day when he saw a sign about a city art contest. The topic was "What My Mom Means to Me." The winner would receive a cash prize! Mario thought about all of the art supplies he could buy if he won. As soon as he got home, he got out his paints and brushes. He thought about everything Mom did for their family. She cooked healthy food for him and his sister. She drove them to swimming classes in the summer. She worked hard so that they could buy new shoes when they grew out of their old ones. Mario smiled and started to paint. Now, he had a new idea for what to do with the money if he won.

1. What is Mario doing?

   painting a picture for an art contest

2. Why does Mom say Mario's art talent is expensive?

   He is always asking her for money for art supplies.

3. What will the winner of the art contest receive?

   a cash prize

4. What does Mario want to do with the prize money?

   buy art supplies

5. What does Mom do for Mario's family?

   cooks healthy food, drives them to swimming classes, buys them new shoes

6. What might be Mario's new idea for the money at the end of the story?

   give the money to his mom

CD-104305 • © Carson-Dellosa

Name _____

Read the story. Then, answer the questions.

Taylor's Tomato Garden

One day, Taylor's class took a field trip to a greenhouse. The students were amazed at how many different plants were growing in the building. There were plump tomatoes and lovely pink orchids. The gardener explained that he kept the greenhouse warm and misty so that the plants could grow better. He said that it was easier to grow plants inside the greenhouse, where they were not in danger from bad weather or pests. When Taylor got home from school, she told her mother all about the greenhouse. She asked if they could build one in their backyard. Wouldn't it be great to have fresh tomatoes year-round? Mom said, "A greenhouse sounds like fun, but it can be a lot of work. Why don't you grow some tomatoes in a pot first to see if you have a green thumb?" Taylor decided to try. She would grow so many tomatoes that they would need a greenhouse to hold them all!

1. What kinds of plants did Taylor's class see?

   tomatoes and orchids

2. Why are greenhouses good places to grow plants?

   They are warm and misty and keep the plants safe from bad weather and pests.

3. What does Taylor want to do?

   build a greenhouse in her backyard

4. What does Mom suggest?

   Taylor should try growing tomatoes in a pot first.

5. What does it mean to have a green thumb?

   to be good at growing things

6. What does Taylor decide to do at the end of the story?

   grow so many tomatoes that they will have to build a greenhouse

CD-104305 • © Carson-Dellosa

Name _____   **Drawing Conclusions**

Read the story. Then, answer the questions.

Family Photos

Valerie's father had accepted a new job across the country, so he would be leaving soon. Valerie and her mother would be staying in their old house until school was out. Valerie would miss her friends when they moved, but she would miss her dad more. Her mother pretended to be cheerful, but Valerie knew she would be lonely too. Sometimes, she caught her mom looking at old photos with a tear in her eye. She decided to make something that would remind both her mom and her dad that they had a strong family. One afternoon, Valerie took the box of family photos up to her room. She cut out two large cardboard hearts. Then, she picked out pictures of herself, her mom, and her dad. She glued the pictures to the hearts. At the top of each heart she wrote "A Family Is Love." Now Dad would have pictures to remember them by, and Mom would not be so sad when she looked at the photos.

1. Why is Valerie's father moving without them?

   He has a new job across the country. Valerie will finish the school year at home.

2. Who will Valerie miss the most?

   her dad

3. Why does Mom pretend to be cheerful?

   She does not want Valerie to be sad.

4. What clues do you have that Mom is not really cheerful?

   She cries when she looks at old photos.

5. Why does Valerie cut out two cardboard hearts?

   She will give one to her mom and one to her dad.

6. Why will Mom be less sad when she looks at photos now?

   They will remind her that their family is strong.

Name _____   **Drawing Conclusions**

Read the story. Then, answer the questions.

Soup Kitchen

Rashad's parents liked to help other people. His mom made recordings of books for the blind, and his dad built new houses for people who could not afford them. Rashad's mother said that they should have Thanksgiving dinner at the soup kitchen. Rashad's dad said that was an excellent idea. Rashad did not know what a soup kitchen was. He liked soup, so maybe it was a place to try lots of different kinds. But they usually ate turkey and stuffing at Thanksgiving. He did not think that soup would taste as good. On Thanksgiving Day, Rashad helped his dad carry boxes to the car. They held canned goods, fresh vegetables, and even a turkey! When they got to the soup kitchen, Rashad discovered that there was more than just soup. The soup kitchen was a place where people could come for dinner if they had no food of their own. Rashad's parents were helping serve dinner. Rashad helped too, and he thought it was the best Thanksgiving ever.

1. How do Rashad's parents help others?

   His mom reads books for the blind, and his dad builds houses.

2. What does Rashad think a soup kitchen is?

   a place to try different kinds of soup

3. What does Rashad's family usually eat at Thanksgiving?

   turkey and stuffing

4. What clues tell you what a *soup kitchen* really is?

   Rashad's parents like to help people, and they carry boxes of food to the car.

5. How do Rashad's parents help at the soup kitchen?

   They bring boxes of food and serve dinner.

6. How can you tell Rashad likes helping people too?

   He thinks that it is the best Thanksgiving ever.

Name _____   **Drawing Conclusions**

Read the story. Then, answer the questions.

Dad's Trumpet

Owen's dad played the trumpet when he was in school. He led the marching band and had a solo in every concert. Owen wanted to play the trumpet too. One day at Grandma's house, he found a dusty case in the closet of his dad's old room. It was Dad's old trumpet! Grandma said that Owen could try it out, so Owen put the instrument to his lips. He blew as hard as he could, but there was no sound. Grandma showed him how to buzz his lips on the mouthpiece, and finally the trumpet made a noise. It sounded nothing like the players Owen had heard in the band. Owen felt sad. He guessed he did not have his dad's talent. He was about to put the trumpet away, when Grandma stopped him. She smiled and said, "You sound just like your dad did when he first started playing. Don't give up yet!"

1. What clues do you have that Owen's dad was a good trumpet player?

   He led the marching band and had a solo in every concert.

2. Why does Owen want to play the trumpet?

   to be like his dad

3. How can you tell that Dad does not play the trumpet anymore?

   The trumpet is at Grandma's house in a dusty case.

4. Why does Owen have a hard time playing the trumpet?

   He does not know how to play yet.

5. Why does Grandma tell Owen not to give up yet?

   His dad had to practice to be a good player, and Owen will too.

6. What do you think Owen will do next?

   He will practice the trumpet so that he can be as good as Dad.

Name _____   **Drawing Conclusions**

Read the story. Then, answer the questions.

The Long Hike

Jackie and her friends decided to go on a hike Saturday morning. They wanted to reach the top of a nearby hill so that they could see the whole town. Her mom asked if she had remembered to pack water and some nuts for the trail. Jackie was in a hurry, but she stopped to pick up a bottle of water and a packet of nuts for her backpack. She thought they would be back before she got thirsty or hungry, but it took them more time to get to the top of the hill than she had expected. When they stopped to rest, she heard her stomach growl. The view was nice. Jackie and her friends sat down and ate a snack. When they finished, they jogged down the trail. When they got to the bottom of the hill, Jackie saw her dad's car pull up. He rolled down the window and said with a smile, "Ready for lunch?"

1. Why do Jackie and her friends want to hike up the hill?

   to see the whole town from the top

2. How can you tell Jackie's parents want her to be careful on the trail?

   Her mom asks if she has water and nuts.

3. What does Jackie take with her?

   her backpack and some water and nuts

4. How can you tell Jackie is glad she brought food and water?

   She hears her stomach growl and stops to have a snack.

5. Why does Jackie's dad come to meet her?

   He thinks that she might be hungry and ready for lunch.

6. What do you think Jackie will do the next time she goes on a hike?

   take food and water with her

Name _____ **Drawing Conclusions**

Read the story. Then, answer the questions.

Gavin's New Pet

Gavin wanted a pet more than anything else in the world. Dogs made him sneeze, and cats made his eyes water. Mom said that he could have a fish, but Gavin wanted something furry to pet. Gavin's teacher brought a hamster to school one day. She said that Harry would live in their classroom, but someone would need to take him home over spring break. Gavin's hand shot up in the air. He knew that Mom would think that Harry was wonderful and allow him to have a hamster of his own. Harry's week at Gavin's house was full of adventure. First, he squirmed away from Gavin's little sister when she tried to pet him. Then, he got out of his cage and hid in Gavin's pile of socks. Finally, he chewed up Gavin's science notebook. At the end of the week, Gavin was happy for Harry to go back to school. He said, "Maybe I'll get a fish after all!"

1. Why can't Gavin get a cat or a dog?

Dogs make him sneeze, and cats make his eyes water.

2. What kind of pet does Gavin want?

something furry to pet

3. Why does Harry have to go home with a student?

The school will be closed over spring break.

4. What does Harry do at Gavin's house?

He squirms away from Gavin's little sister, hides in Gavin's socks, and chews up Gavin's science notebook.

5. Why is Gavin happy to take Harry back to school?

Harry is harder to take care of than Gavin had thought.

6. Why does Gavin decide to get a fish after all?

Fish are less trouble to take care of. They stay in their bowls and cannot chew anything of Gavin's.

96 CD-104305 • © Carson-Dellosa

Name _____ **Predicting**

Read the story. Then, answer the questions.

Predicting

A. Sandra's mother offered to help her get ready for the new school year. Sandra had grown a full inch taller over the summer. Her shoes were too tight, and her pants were almost above her ankles.

1. What do you think Sandra and her mother will do?

shop for new school clothes

2. Which clues helped you decide?

Sandra had grown taller over the summer, her shoes were too tight, and her pants were too short.

B. When Betsy got home from school, she could not find her cat. Betsy called out her cat's name, but her cat did not come. Betsy looked in her closet. She looked under her bed. Just then, Betsy heard her dad drive up. He was home from work. Betsy was glad her dad was home.

1. What do you think Betsy will do?

ask her dad to help look for her cat

2. Which clues helped you decide?

She looked in many places but couldn't find her cat; her dad was home now.

C. Mandy tried out for the school track team. She wore her favorite shoes and came in first in her race. The gym teacher posted the results the day after the tryouts. Mandy raced to the gym to see the list of who had made the team.

1. What do you think will happen next?

Mandy will make the track team.

2. Which clues helped you decide?

Mandy won her race.

CD-104305 • © Carson-Dellosa 97

Name _____ **Predicting**

Read the story. Then, answer the questions.

Predicting

A. Miguel needed to write a book report. He finished reading the book and began to plan his paper. The report was worth two test grades, so it was important for him to do well. Miguel's mom said that he had a phone call. It was his friend Tony, who wanted to play video games.

1. What do you think will happen next?

Miguel will finish the book report instead of going to Tony's house.

2. Which clues helped you decide?

He is making notes for the report, so he wants to do well.

B. Timothy laid his head on his desk. His face felt hot, and the desk was nice and cool. Timothy's class was supposed to have an ice cream party that afternoon. Timothy thought the ice cream would feel good to his sore throat. Just then, his teacher said that she thought Timothy should go to the nurse's office.

1. What do you think will happen next?

The nurse will send him home. He will miss the party.

2. Which clues helped you decide?

His face is hot and his throat is sore, so he is too sick to stay at school.

C. Lynn and her brother Trey decided to go hiking. They wore sturdy shoes and light clothing. They put on hats and plenty of sunscreen. They had just reached the top of a tall, rocky hill when they heard a clap of thunder. The sky grew dark. Trey spotted a cave in the side of the hill.

1. What do you think will happen next?

stay in the cave until the storm passes

2. Which clues helped you decide?

The sky is dark and they heard thunder, so it is going to storm. Trey saw a cave in the side of the hill.

98 CD-104305 • © Carson-Dellosa

Name _____ **Predicting**

Read the story. Then, answer the questions.

Predicting

A. Angel's teacher told the class to close their math books. They were having a pop test! Angel was surprised. She was happy she had studied the chapter the night before. She had not understood the problems in class, so she had asked her mother for extra help. She took out a sheet of paper and wrote her name at the top.

1. What do you think will happen next?

Angel will do well on the test.

2. Which clues helped you decide?

She had studied the chapter the night before.

B. Brian came home from school and prepared himself a sandwich. He put some slices of meat and cheese on it with extra mustard. Brian put his sandwich on a plate and took it to the living room. He thought he would watch his favorite TV show while he ate. His dog came in to see what Brian was doing. Brian set his sandwich on the table and went back into the kitchen for a glass of milk.

1. What do you think will happen next?

Brian's dog will steal his sandwich.

2. Which clues helped you decide?

Brian has left his sandwich behind to get a glass of milk.

C. Sarah went to her uncle's farm to visit her cousin, Kami. Sarah and Kami were the same age and wore the same size. Sometimes, people thought they were twins! Kami wanted to go fishing, so she told Sarah to put on old jeans. Then, Sarah realized she had forgotten her suitcase.

1. What do you think will happen next?

Kami will lend Sarah some old clothes.

2. Which clues helped you decide?

The two cousins wore the same size.

CD-104305 • © Carson-Dellosa 99

Name _____ | Predicting |

Read the story. Then, answer the questions.

Predicting

A. Raul wanted to earn money this summer. He was tired of asking for change to buy comic books and candy. His best friend, Shane, lived next door. Shane and his family were going to be gone all summer. Shane's family could not travel on the plane with their two dogs.

1. What do you think Raul will do?

    offer to take care of Shane's dogs for the summer

2. Which clues helped you decide?

    He wants to earn money over the summer. Shane's
    family could not take the dogs on vacation with them.

B. Jan's family was moving to a new town with their orange and white cat. Sadly, the cat ran away when they were moving boxes from the truck to the house. Two weeks later, the cat still had not returned. Jan was very sad. She missed her cat. Her new friend Laura, who lived next door, called Jan one morning to say that she had just seen an orange and white cat in her yard.

1. What do you think will happen next?

    Jan will find her cat.

2. Which clues helped you decide?

    Laura saw the same color cat in her yard.

C. Kelsey wanted to surprise her mom with a cake. With Grandma's help, she mixed the ingredients and put the batter in a pan. She turned on the oven and put the pan inside. She set a timer and waited for the cake to bake. Kelsey's mom came home early and called, "What is that wonderful smell?"

1. What do you think will happen next?

    Kelsey will surprise her mom with the cake.

2. Which clues helped you decide?

    Kelsey's mom came home early. Kelsey is baking the
    cake as a surprise.

100   CD-104305 • © Carson-Dellosa

Name _____ | Predicting |

Read the story. Then, answer the questions.

Predicting

A. Jason stood at the top of the ladder to the diving board. His knees felt wobbly, and his hands were sweaty. He walked out onto the board. It was a long way down. Just then, he heard his sister shout, "Come on, Jason! You can do it!" He took a deep breath.

1. What do you think Jason will do?

    He will dive off the diving board.

2. Which clues helped you decide?

    His sister shouted that she knew he could do it. He took
    a deep breath, so he is preparing to dive off.

B. Stephen's stepdad was working late every night. He had not gotten home before dark for the past month. Stephen noticed that the yard was covered in dead leaves. He knew his mom did not like it. She had hurt her leg and could not stand up for very long. Stephen wanted to help.

1. What do you think Stephen will do?

    rake the yard and bag up the leaves

2. Which clues helped you decide?

    His stepdad is working late, his mom hurt her leg, and
    Stephen wants to help them.

C. Lindsey took piano lessons. She liked to play for her mom every night after dinner. Sometimes, her friends came over to sing while she played. Lindsey's piano teacher was having a party for all of her students the next week. She wanted all of her students to play for each other, and one would win a prize.

1. What do you think will happen next?

    Lindsey will play well and win a prize.

2. Which clues helped you decide?

    Lindsey plays piano often, so she is probably very good.

CD-104305 • © Carson-Dellosa   101

Name _____ | Predicting |

Read the story. Then, answer the questions.

Predicting

A. Tara found a pair of sunglasses on the bus. They were bright pink with red lightning bolts on the earpieces. Tara felt like a rock star wearing them. After lunch, Tara put on the sunglasses to go out for recess. An older girl ran up to her and said, "Excuse me, but I think that those are mine." Tara's heart sank.

1. What do you think Tara will do?

    explain that she found the sunglasses on the bus, give them back

2. Which clues helped you to decide?

    Tara's heart sank, so she knows she should give them back.

B. Ray wanted to play football more than anything else in the world. There was a new team starting in his neighborhood, and he wanted to try out. His family was concerned that if Ray joined the team, he would not have time to do his homework. His family wanted Ray to have fun, but they also wanted him to do well in school. Ray was sure that he would have time to do his homework and play on the team.

1. What do you think will happen next?

    Ray's family will let him play football if he keeps his grades up.

2. Which clues helped you to decide?

    They want him to have fun and do well in school.

C. Ivy's grandmother was celebrating her 70th birthday soon. Ivy wanted to get her grandmother a special gift, but she had spent her money on new books instead. Ivy loved reading books about Mexico. Her grandmother had come from Mexico, and she used to read to Ivy when she was little. Lately, her grandmother's eyesight had been failing, and she could no longer see the words on the page.

1. What do you think Ivy will do?

    offer to read to her grandmother as a special gift

2. Which clues helped you to decide?

    Ivy's grandmother used to read to her, but now she cannot see.
    Ivy and her grandmother both like to read about Mexico.

102   CD-104305 • © Carson-Dellosa

Name _____ | Predicting |

Read the story. Then, answer the questions.

Predicting

A. Felipe was a new boy in Ethan's class. He did not speak much English, and the teacher could tell that he needed a little extra help. She asked Ethan to help Felipe understand the words in their homework. Ethan went over to Felipe's house after school. He noticed that Felipe's room was covered in posters of soccer players. "Wow!" said Ethan. "I have always wanted to learn to play soccer."

1. What do you think will happen next?

    Felipe will teach Ethan how to play soccer in exchange for
    helping him with his homework.

2. Which clues helped you decide?

    Ethan is helping Felipe with English. Felipe has soccer
    posters, and Ethan wants to learn to play soccer.

B. Bridget's mother worked in a restaurant. She often had to work late. Bridget thought Mom would enjoy working in an office more, but Mom did not know how to use a computer. Bridget saw a flyer at the library about a computer class for adults. The class met on Saturday mornings, when Bridget was usually at dance class. If Mom signed up for the class, there would be no one to watch Bridget's little brother.

1. What do you think Bridget will do?

    offer to watch her brother so that Mom can take the class

2. Which clues helped you decide?

    Bridget wants Mom to work in an office, and she finds a
    computer class for Mom to take.

CD-104305 • © Carson-Dellosa   103
